WORSHIP AND WITNESS

BECOMING A **GREAT COMMISSION** WORSHIPER

DAVID WHEELER AND VERNON M. WHALEY

LIFEWAY PRESS®
NASHVILLE, TENNESSEE

Published by LifeWay Press®
© 2012 David Wheeler and Vernon M. Whaley

ISBN 978-1-4158-4856-2
Item 005565320

Dewey decimal classification: 264
Subject headings: WORSHIP \ EVANGELISTIC WORK

Unless indicated otherwise, all Scripture quotations are taken from the
Holman Christian Standard Bible®, copyright © 1999, 2000, 2002, 2003,
2009 by Holman Bible Publishers. Used by permission. Holman Christian
Standard Bible®, Holman CSB®, and HCSB® are federally registered trade-
marks of Holman Bible Publishers. Scripture quotations marked NIV are
taken from the Holy Bible, New International Version, copyright © 1973,
1978, 1984 by International Bible Society. Scripture quotations marked
ESV are taken from The Holy Bible, English Standard Version, copyright
© 2000, 2001 by Crossway Bibles, a division of Good News Publishers.

To order additional copies of this resource, write to LifeWay Church
Resources Customer Service; One LifeWay Plaza; Nashville, TN 37234-0113;
fax (615) 251-5933; phone toll free (800) 458-2772; order online at
www.lifeway.com; e-mail *orderentry@lifeway.com;* or visit the LifeWay
Christian Store serving you.

Printed in the United States of America

Adult Ministry Publishing
LifeWay Church Resources
One LifeWay Plaza
Nashville, TN 37234-0152

CONTENTS

THE AUTHORS

DAVID WHEELER is a professor of evangelism at Liberty University and Liberty Baptist Theological Seminary. He also serves as the director of applied ministries and the associate director of the center for church planting and the center for ministry training. He coauthored *Evangelism Is ... How to Share Jesus with Passion and Confidence, The Great Commission to Worship*, and *Growing Disciples: Minister to Others*.

VERNON M. WHALEY is the dean of the Liberty University School of Music and a professor of music and worship at Liberty Baptist Theological Seminary. He is also the president of Integra Music Group and the author of *Understanding Music and Worship in the Local Church. The Dynamics of Corporate Worship, Called to Worship*, and *Worship Through the Ages*, as well as the coauthor of *The Great Commission to Worship*.

PREFACE

A PERSONAL NOTE
FROM DAVID WHEELER

My life radically changed as a 17-year-old high-school junior when my youth leader gave me a copy of the Roman Road gospel presentation and dared me to share it with at least one unsaved friend. I was three weeks into a dating relationship with a beautiful girl named Debbi. One evening she came over to my house for a romantic night of basketball. At some point the Holy Spirit reminded me about the challenge, so I took the plunge: "Debbi, do you go to church?"

She quickly answered, "No, not really." At this point I was sweating profusely and shaking violently in my tennis shoes. But I mustered enough courage to ask, "Well, you're a Christian, aren't you?"

She answered, "No, not that I'm aware of."

For the first time in my life, I began to share the gospel, walking through the Roman Road presentation my youth leader had given me. I'm certain I butchered it, yet the Holy Spirit moved, and Debbi surrendered her life to Christ.

My life has never been the same. Debbi and I were eventually married after our final year of college. In addition, I was awakened to the call of the Great Commission. For the first time I felt like a real disciple of Christ, not merely a spectator watching Him work from a distance.

All of this launched me on a mission to understand the purpose of the Christian life. For a long time I argued that evangelism is our whole reason to exist as believers. After all, Jesus said He came "to seek and to save the lost" (Luke 19:10).

At this point God brought Vernon Whaley back into my life. We had known each other in high school and college, and now we were colleagues at Liberty University, where he taught worship classes and I taught evangelism classes. Over time we sparred back and forth on the purpose of the Christian life. While I was certain it was evangelism, he argued it was worship.

In 2007 David and I were traveling together to a missions meeting in Atlanta when David asked, "Which came first—the chicken or the egg?"

"What are you talking about?" I replied.

"Evangelism or worship—which comes first?"

"Oh," I said. "Are we going to fight that battle again?" We did.

As we drove down the road, we thoroughly discussed our positions on evangelism and worship. We had difficulty finding common ground. David had been around some worship-musicians who misunderstood their calling. They were all about the process, planning, preparation, and presentation of worship music, but they had little interest in evangelism.

On the other hand, I had been around preachers who marginalized worship to focus on evangelism. However, their real interest was in exalting their reputation by engaging in church politics and adding to their membership rolls.

Unfortunately, both of these extremes are unbiblical, and they're deadly to a church's ministry. We kept arguing until one of us asked, "Which is most important—the Great Commission or the Great Commandment—making disciples or loving the Lord with all your heart, soul, mind, and strength?" Because of our biases and misunderstandings, neither of us could answer with any serious integrity. I think that's when the Holy Spirit began working.

On the way back home, we discussed the issue again, but this time we began with the Bible instead of misguided proponents of worship or evangelism. We talked about the importance of the Great Commission to the early church and the way it approached Kingdom work. The early disciples loved the Lord and sought to worship Him and obey His every word. Because of that love, they wanted to lead people from every tribe, tongue, and nation to become worshipers of the living Lord as well. They were equally committed to worship and evangelism. They were Great Commission worshipers.

This Bible study is the outcome of our heated discussions about the purpose of the Christian life. Which is more important—the Great Commission or the Great Commandment? Both are equally important, and both are divine commandments. So how do we develop a strategy for evangelism that doesn't exclude our responsibility to worship? And how do we involve ourselves in worship without ignoring or marginalizing the biblical mandate to evangelize? This study will examine these questions in order to present a biblical view of what it means to be a Great Commission worshiper—someone who understands what it means to be an authentic, reproducing disciple and worshiper of Jesus Christ.

The early church lived out its commitment to both worship and evangelism so passionately and persistently that its detractors accused it of turning the world upside down (see Acts 17:6). Unfortunately, the modern church has lost its two-pronged compass of exalting Christ in worship and reproducing His kingdom through biblical evangelism. The aim of this study is to help God's people recapture their Great Commission calling and to once again become worshipers who turn the world upside down for the glory of God and the testimony of Jesus Christ.

EXPRESSING GREAT COMMISSION WORSHIP

At the end of each day's lesson you'll have the opportunity to respond to what you've learned about Great Commission worship through activities called Today's Evangelism Expression and Today's Worship Expression. These activities will drive home the key elements of Great Commission worship and will help you take concrete steps to become a Great Commission worshiper. You'll be asked to answer questions, make lists, develop testimonies, and reach out to God and others to express the principles of Great Commission worship in your daily life and witness. Because these activities require more space than the other learning activities you'll complete throughout this workbook, you'll find it helpful to use a separate journal or notebook to complete your Evangelism and Worship Expressions each day.

GREAT COMMISSION WORSHIP IS FORMATIONAL

Making pottery has been a respected profession and hobby for thousands of years, and it continues to be an important part of many cultures around the world.

While the most basic tool for any maker of good pottery is the hand, there are a variety of implements and materials that come into play. Fire is the agent by which clay and other materials are changed into earthenware, stoneware, or porcelain, which means a kiln is a necessary device. People also use wheels, turntables, knives, rollers, and more. Of course, the most important tool is the mind of the potter himself—his creativity, skill, patience, and attention to detail.

Perhaps what's most appealing about making pottery is the dual nature of the craft. The process is both artistic and practical. It starts with raw materials that are seemingly mundane—clay, dirt, minerals, and more—and ends with the formation of something practical and often beautiful.

It's no wonder, then, that the Bible frequently uses pottery to illustrate the spiritual formation of both individuals and communities. After all, we as human beings are raw and filthy in our sin, but we're also created in the image of God and possess the potential for beauty.

In His wisdom God provides many tools and methods for shaping us into His image and making us useful for His purposes. As we'll see this week, the proper worship of God is an effective tool for tapping our potential and forming us into useful vessels that reflect His glory.

DAY 1

GREAT COMMISSION WORSHIP

What's more important in the life of a Christian—worship or evangelism?
That's a tough question.

On one hand, much of what we do as Christians every week is considered worship.
We pray to God throughout the day. We listen to worship CDs. We sing hymns
and songs of praise at church. More importantly, the Bible repeatedly commands
us to worship God, using words like "Praise the LORD, all nations!" (Ps. 117:1).

On the other hand, evangelism is an unquestionably vital part of the Christian life.
Just the idea of outreach feels weighty and important because eternity is at stake
for billions of people around the world. That's why we learn the Roman Road and
invite our neighbors to church. That's why we go on mission trips and proclaim
the gospel of Jesus Christ.

So is it worship or evangelism? Which one is our greatest calling that deserves
our most fervent effort?

How do you answer the previous question? Why?

If you're having trouble deciding whether worship or evangelism represents our
primary purpose as believers, you're actually on the right track. That's because
worship and evangelism aren't separate elements—or at least they shouldn't be.
In reality, they're unified expressions of obedience to God, both of which deserve
our full attention as we seek to follow Jesus and help others follow Him as well.

MISCONCEPTIONS

The reason we often perceive a separation between worship and evangelism is
that many Christians (and many churches) possess a false view of each experience.
There's a disconnect between the biblical view of worship and evangelism and the
way we often carry out those activities.

For example, many Christians' idea of worship is limited to an emotional high on Sunday mornings, yet during the week they ignore Jesus' mandate to go and make disciples of all nations (see Matt. 28:19). At the same time, many Christians feel pressure to try and "bring people to Jesus." However, without grounding their efforts in genuine worship, they win converts but fail to make disciples who are true worshipers.

During what seasons of life have you had passionate, meaningful experiences of worshiping God?

During what seasons of life have you been motivated and successful in sharing your faith?

The truth is, modern believers (and modern churches) aren't worshiping well, nor are we doing a good job of making disciples. We've created a false dichotomy between those elements, and both have suffered.

The purpose of this study is to offer a biblical understanding of worship and evangelism as united expressions of obedience to God. Throughout the next six weeks we'll also shed light on how God intended His followers to express both callings as we seek to multiply the kingdom of God.

A NEW DEFINITION

Both evangelism and worship are expressions of a life totally committed to Jesus Christ. As such, they allow us to live out our primary purpose as followers of Jesus. That purpose is defined well by the first line of the Westminster Shorter Confession: "Man's chief end is to glorify God, and to enjoy Him forever."[1]

Read Romans 11:33-36 and Ephesians 3:14-21. What does it mean to glorify God?

When have you recently concentrated on bringing glory to God? What was the result?

The purpose of a believer's life is to glorify God. We worship so that God can be eternally exalted among the nations. We bring people to Christ for the same reason. When we live surrendered, obedient lives that seek God's glory, we offer open invitations for others to become worshipers of our great God. Evangelism and worship are therefore uniquely related. Evangelism ignites a holistic lifestyle of worship, and worship of the one true God leads to evangelism.

Jesus issued two commands that define our calling to worship and evangelism. The first is the Great Commission:

> Jesus came near and said to them, "All authority has been given to Me in heaven and on earth. Go, therefore, and make disciples of all nations, baptizing them in the name of the Father and of the Son and of the Holy Spirit, teaching them to observe everything I have commanded you. And remember, I am with you always, to the end of the age."
>
> Matthew 28:18-20

This was Jesus' final command before ascending to heaven, and it assured His followers of His power and His presence. He instructed them to go and make disciples, baptizing and teaching them. In doing so, they would bring glory to God by leading more and more people to worship Him.

How does evangelism bring glory to God?

How have you seen evangelism result in God's being glorified?

Jesus' also instructed His disciples in what is now called the Great Commandment:

> "Love the Lord your God with all your heart, with all your soul, and with all your mind." This is the greatest and most important command. The second is like it: "Love your neighbor as yourself." All the Law and the Prophets depend on these two commands.
>
> Matthew 22:37-40

Jesus' words express the heart of both worship and evangelism. He called us to glorify God with unyielding allegiance, but our worship isn't complete unless we also love our neighbor. If we fall in love with Christ and seek to glorify His name, we'll also love others and lead them to worship with us.

Biblical worship, therefore, is a passionate response of devotion and obedience to God, and it results in active participation in the Great Commission. Neither evangelism nor worship is an isolated religious activity; both combine to form a lifestyle that seeks to glorify God by joining Him on mission every day.

In the weeks ahead we'll learn more about how we can bring glory to God by becoming Great Commission worshipers.

Summarize the connection between worship and evangelism.

How does this connection bring glory to God?

In your own words, what does it mean to live as a Great Commission worshiper?

If you're feeling some pressure to figure out how worship and evangelism should fit together in your Christian walk, take a deep breath. The good news is that God wants to use His followers to fulfill His purposes. In fact, He's already in the process of perfecting you for the task of Great Commission worship.

Through this study you'll simply align yourself with what God has already been doing in your life. As you do so, you'll discover more and more the power and privilege involved in Great Commission worship.

TODAY'S EVANGELISM EXPRESSION

Each day's lesson will end with an Evangelism Expression and a Worship Expression, which are designed to help you live out what you're learning about Great Commission worship. You'll need a separate journal or notebook to complete these activities each day.

Spend a few minutes contemplating your life before you experienced the saving power of Jesus Christ. Record your answers to the following questions.
• What were your primary influences and motivations during that time period?
• What were your biggest dreams?
• What were your deepest fears?
• List three words that describe your life before you became a Christian.

TODAY'S WORSHIP EXPRESSION

Reread the Great Commission (Matt. 28:18-20) and the Great Commandment (Matt. 22:37-40). As you pray throughout the day, ask God to grant you a passionate desire to obey these commands and to help others do the same.

DAY 2

THE GOD WE WORSHIP

Worship and evangelism are important practices for churches and individual Christians. We've always understood that. What's revolutionary is the idea that worship and evangelism are pieces of the same whole rather than competing activities in our lives. That's the essence of Great Commission worship, and that's what we'll explore throughout this study.

As we dig deeper into these concepts, we'll focus on several outcomes of Great Commission worship—what happens in the lives of believers when biblical worship joins forces with biblical evangelism. There are five of these outcomes: Great Commission worship is formational, transformational, relational, missional, and reproducible.

We'll use the remainder of this week's lessons to explore the first outcome: the role Great Commission worship plays in our spiritual formation. Worship and evangelism aren't static experiences. We don't engage them and then walk away unaffected, like taking a dip in a pool.

Rather, Great Commission worship is formational. It sculpts us and shapes us into something new. The more we glorify God through worship and evangelism, the more we're conformed to His image. This happens every time we feast on God's Word, worship the God of the Word, apply His Word to our lives, share the gospel with a friend, and experience God's mercies new every morning.

How has your spiritual growth been impacted by worship?

How has your spiritual growth been impacted by evangelism?

To understand how Great Commission worship forms us more and more closely into the image of God, we need to highlight a few things about His nature.

TWO QUALITIES

One thing we need to come to grips with is the fact that God is transcendent. This means He's above all created things. He's the ruler of the universe and beyond our limited experience as human beings. He transcends what we can comprehend.

Read the following verses and record how they contribute to your understanding of God's transcendence.

Isaiah 40:21-23

Isaiah 55:8-9

Psalm 99:1-3

God is worthy of our worship. He's great and marvelous, magnificent and holy, sufficient and self-sustaining, beyond our ability to understand or explain, and the Creator of all things. The list can go on and on. Recognizing God's transcendence makes us aware of our lowly human status in comparison, and we naturally respond with praise.

Amazingly, even though God is transcendent, He's also immanent. That means He's involved in all parts of the universe, including every facet of our lives. Although God is high above us, He wants to draw near His children in a close, personal relationship. God actively takes a role in our everyday experiences. He loves us, nurtures us, and provides for us.

Read the following verses and record how they contribute to your understanding of God's immanence.

Jeremiah 29:11-13

Ezekiel 34:11-15

Matthew 7:7-11

God is our Father, Shepherd, friend, companion, hope, and help. Again, the list can go on and on. Both transcendence and immanence describe our relationship with our holy, all-knowing, and all-loving God. Both qualities lead us to worship, and both qualities inspire us to proclaim God's nature to those who have yet to experience Him firsthand.

A TWO-WAY STREET

An important principle we need to understand about God is that our relationship with Him is a two-way street. God doesn't just receive our worship, store it away, and at the end of the day record the number of times we pray and exalt Him. God isn't selfish. He doesn't need us to brag on Him. He isn't a self-centered deity who demands memorized, habitual, or obligatory prayers.

Rather, God always responds to our worship of Him. We praise Him because we recognize and adore Him as the transcendent, immanent, omniscient, omnipresent, and omnipotent God who loves and cares for us. We share our testimony with others for the same reasons. And when we do so, God responds by nurturing, developing, and cultivating our relationship with Him.

What kinds of experiences cause you to feel closer to God? Why?

Remember that we glorify God not only by praising Him but also by obeying Him in evangelism and other types of ministry. When we worship God in faith with love, devotion, obedience, and service, He responds to us by giving us His grace, love, devotion, companionship, and care. As we spend time with Him in worship, He increases our desire to worship. As He increases that desire, we worship more deeply and sincerely. In other words, God uses our worship to shape us and form us into His likeness. Great Commission worship is formational.

A CASE STUDY

The life of the Old Testament prophet Jeremiah is a great example of formational worship. God commissioned Jeremiah to proclaim to the ungrateful, ungodly, self-consumed nation of Judah that because of its sins, it would reap grief, destruction, heartache, and devastation.

The only child of a temple priest, Jeremiah was molded by godly influences. He had a genuine love for God and hated idol worship. His strong messages exhibited disdain for the dishonest policies of the monarchs, making him unpopular with the evil kings and their followers. On more than one occasion he ran for his life. Even so, Jeremiah never lost his sense of calling. His commitment to the worship of Jehovah shaped a simple, honest, and consistent trust in God. Jeremiah's worship shaped his relationship with God in three specific ways.

1. GOD SHAPED JEREMIAH'S LANGUAGE.

> The LORD reached out His hand,
> touched my mouth, and told me:
> I have now filled your mouth with My words.
> See, I have appointed you today
> over nations and kingdoms
> to uproot and tear down
> to destroy and demolish,
> to build and plant.
>
> Jeremiah 1:9-10

How have you experienced God's direction when you shared your faith or talked with others about Him?

2. GOD SHAPED JEREMIAH'S LIFE. God selected Jeremiah to devote his life to a specific task:

> I chose you before I formed you in the womb;
> I set you apart before you were born.
> I appointed you a prophet to the nations.
>
> Jeremiah 1:5

Jeremiah's worship prompted him to live a life of obedience. His faith drove him to a life of obedient commitment and service to the One he loved most. His faithfulness energized his courage to always do what was right. God used what seemed to be unbearable circumstances to shape Jeremiah's character, integrity, and faith. In response, Jeremiah's worship of the Lord deepened.

3. GOD SHAPED JEREMIAH'S MINISTRY. At the moment Jeremiah accepted God's plan for his life, God began to mold the young prophet into a man of courage. Jeremiah lived and experienced formational worship, and God gave him the ability to carry out the tasks before him. God promised him:

Today, I am the One who has made you a fortified city, an iron pillar, and bronze walls against the whole land—against the kings of Judah, its officials, its priests, and the population. They will fight against you but never prevail over you, since I am with you to rescue you.

Jeremiah 1:18-19

Each time Jeremiah received a word from God, his understanding about God grew, and his worship of God deepened. In the same way, the more he shared God's words with the people who needed to hear them, the more the process shaped his life. That's the power of a life formed by Great Commission worship.

How have you seen God use your experiences with worship and evangelism to shape you for ministry?

TODAY'S EVANGELISM EXPRESSION

Spend a few minutes contemplating the events and experiences that preceded your salvation. Record your answers to the following questions.

- When did you begin to realize that your lifestyle wasn't working—that you were unhappy and unsatisfied?
- How did you attempt to find happiness and satisfaction? What happened?
- Which people served as God's representatives in your life? What did they say?

TODAY'S WORSHIP EXPRESSION

Take several moments throughout the day to express your praise for God's transcendent nature. Speak to Him about the marvelous things He's done, both in the world and in your personal experiences. In those same moments also praise God for His immanence and involvement in your life. Thank Him for the ways He nurtures and sustains your relationship with Him.

DAY 3

JESUS: THE FOCUS OF WORSHIP

For Christians, the Christmas season is a time of great joy as we celebrate the birth of our Savior, Jesus Christ. At the same time, we also experience a mixture of sadness and frustration when we see much of our culture celebrate "the holidays" in ways that exclude any mention of Jesus. We feel the tragedy of seeing Christ taken out of Christmas.

In what other areas does our culture attempt to restrict or remove the influence of Jesus Christ and His Word?

Just as it's a mistake to omit Jesus as the reason for the Christmas season, it's also damaging to forget that He's the central figure involved in our worship and evangelism. Indeed, biblical worship and evangelism must be centered on Jesus Christ.

We're not talking about an abstract idea of Jesus or a vague recognition that He's important. Rather, Great Commission worship is all about the concrete reality of Jesus. He's the Messiah who's worthy of all honor and praise, and He's the living Savior to whom all our evangelistic energy must point.

What happens when churches and Christians attempt to worship and evangelize without clearly pointing to the Person of Jesus?

To continue exploring Great Commission worship on firm footing, let's spend some time solidifying our understanding of and appreciation for Jesus Christ.

ETERNAL GOD AND SON

When it comes to capturing the full measure of Jesus' nature and ministry on earth, few passages of Scripture are more helpful than John 1.

Read John 1:1-18. What do you enjoy most about these verses? Why?

What images stand out to you most in these verses? What do those images communicate about Jesus?

The most important thing we need to understand about Jesus is that He's God. He's the eternal Creator and Sustainer of the universe. As John wrote in verse 1:

> The Word was with God,
> and the Word was God.

Therefore, when we pray, sing songs, and glorify God through obedient worship, we're glorifying Jesus Christ. He's the true Light of the world who deserves all praise. In fact, we were expressly created for the purpose of worshiping Him.

In the same way, evangelism doesn't involve talking with people about concepts or vague ideas of the divine. Instead, it's an opportunity to glorify Jesus by sharing our personal experiences with Him—the Creator of the universe—and by inviting others to encounter that Creator for themselves.

How does worshiping Jesus help our efforts to share our faith with others?

How does sharing our faith enhance our efforts to praise and honor Jesus?

SUFFERING SERVANT

When we understand that Jesus is God and the Creator of the universe, we should be properly shocked at the idea that He desires a personal relationship with us, His creations. And we should be flabbergasted by these words from John 1:14:

> The Word became flesh
> and took up residence among us.
> We observed His glory,
> the glory as the One and Only Son from the Father,
> full of grace and truth.

The message of the gospel is that human beings were lost and broken because of our sin. We had no way to reestablish our connection with God—the connection we'd severed through our rebellion—and yet God's love for us was unchanged. His desire for a relationship with us inspired Him to step out of eternal glory and into the mess and muck of our sinful world.

That's Jesus. He became one of us in order to save all of us once and for all.

Read Philippians 2:5-11. What's shocking about these verses? Why?

How do these verses inspire both evangelism and worship by Jesus' followers?

Not only did Jesus Christ manifest Himself in our world as our Savior, but He also demonstrated the extremity of His love by allowing Himself to be killed on a cross for our sakes. He died, and yet He conquered death by rising from the grave on the third day. In doing so, He made a way for us to partake in His resurrection and experience eternal life with Him.

HEAD OF THE CHURCH

Jesus is no longer physically manifested on earth, yet He hasn't abandoned us. He continues to work on our behalf through His church.

What's your reaction when you hear the word *church*? Why?

What have you liked best about your experiences with churches in recent years? What's made you most disappointed about those experiences?

What we call the church isn't a building. The church consists of all of the men, women, and children who've relinquished control of their lives to Jesus Christ. The church is made up of human beings, yet the entire structure is supported and given life by Jesus.

The apostle Paul helped us understand these concepts by painting a picture of the church as an enormous body that lives and works in the world. He pictured Christ as the Head who directs and rules that body to accomplish what He wants.

Read Romans 12:4-5 and Ephesians 1:22-23. In your own words, summarize the relationship between Jesus and the church.

How does the church help us glorify Jesus through worship and evangelism?

Jesus loved us enough to create us in His image (see Gen. 1:26) and to develop a relationship with us. He valued that relationship so much that He not only forgives our sin but also sacrificed Himself to save us from our sin and rebellion. Even today He works through His church to accomplish all we were created for.

OUR ULTIMATE GOAL

This week we're focusing on the fact that genuine experiences with Great Commission worship are formational: they sculpt and shape us into something new. Here's the best news: the something new we're being shaped into is actually Jesus. As we worship God and share our faith, we're molded more and more into the image of Christ.

Look at the apostle Paul's words in Galatians 3:27: "As many of you as have been baptized into Christ have put on Christ like a garment." When we experience salvation through Jesus, we're given His righteousness "like a garment" to cover our sinfulness. This event is called justification.

But justification is only the beginning. As we begin obeying God through worship, evangelism, and ministry, we start the process of being conformed to His image. Through that process, called sanctification, our very essence is shaped into something new and wonderful that's more and more like Jesus. That's God's plan for us: "Those He foreknew He also predestined to be conformed to the image of His Son, so that He would be the firstborn among many brothers" (Rom. 8:29).

What's your reaction to the previous statements? Why?

In what ways are you more like Jesus today than when you first encountered Him?

Great Commission worship is the proper response to who Jesus is and everything He's done on our behalf. No other message is more important for us to share, and no other person is more worthy of our praise.

TODAY'S EVANGELISM EXPRESSION

Think about your first encounters with Jesus.
- When did you first hear the story of Jesus' life, death, and resurrection? How did you respond?
- When did you first experience Jesus on a personal level? What happened, and how did you respond?
- Why did you decide to give up control of your life to follow Jesus?

TODAY'S WORSHIP EXPRESSION

Go through your personal music collection or browse through songs online until you find a song that expresses your feelings about Jesus and what He's done for you. Commit to sing that song throughout the day (move it to the top of your playlist, for example) as a way of recognizing and reflecting on your gratitude.

DAY 4

WORSHIP IS SHAPED BY SCRIPTURE

The Jewish psychiatrist Viktor Frankl was arrested and imprisoned by the Nazis in World War II. Assigned to the concentration camp at Auschwitz, he was stripped of everything he owned, including his life's work—a book he'd been writing on life's meaning. Frankl had hidden the treasured manuscript in the lining of his coat, but the Nazis forced everyone in the camp to give up their clothes, depriving him of his only intellectual and emotional comfort. He began asking himself whether life was ultimately void of any meaning. He lost hope.

In time, however, the Nazis handed Frankl another set of clothing. "Instead of the many pages of my manuscript," he later wrote, "I found in the pocket of the newly acquired coat a single page torn out of a Hebrew prayer book." Written on that single page were words from the Shema Yisrael, the Jewish confession of faith: "Listen, Israel: The Lord our God, the Lord is One. Love the Lord your God with all your heart, with all your soul, and with all your strength" (Deut. 6:4-5).

This was no coincidence. Through this Scripture God was teaching Frankl how to live his commitment to God. He was instilling in Frankl's heart a reason to survive. His purpose in life—to glorify God—hadn't changed.[2]

Take a moment to identify instances in which words—Bible verses, song lyrics, quotations, literature, and so on—have influenced your life in a major way. Name three examples.

1.

2.

3.

How have your experiences with the Bible changed from the time you first encountered it until today?

We've discussed the fact that Great Commission worship is formational for those who experience it. Let's focus on the role God's Word plays in that process.

SCRIPTURE IS FORMATIONAL

At any given time there are literally millions of books in print that are circulating throughout the world. Most of us are lucky if we can find time to read dozens of those books each year—and very lucky if more than a handful of those books impact us in a meaningful way.

The Bible is different. It's set apart from all other published material because it stands as the very Word of God that He gave to guide us through life. The Bible isn't passive, as all other books are. We don't read it so much as we experience its power. That's why the author of Hebrews wrote the following.

> The word of God is living and effective and sharper than any double-edged sword, penetrating as far as the separation of soul and spirit, joints and marrow. It is able to judge the ideas and thoughts of the heart. No creature is hidden from Him, but all things are naked and exposed to the eyes of Him to whom we must give an account.
>
> Hebrews 4:12-13

What does verse 12 mean when it says God's Word is "living and effective"?

When have you been penetrated or cut by the power of God's Word? What happened?

The use of the word *sword* in verse 12 is interesting. It implies that the Bible functions much like a surgeon's scalpel when a doctor carefully locates the place for surgery, makes an incision, penetrates deep into the flesh, and skillfully cuts out infection or diseased tissue. In the same way, God's Word is a tool that clears away rough edges and shapes someone into the image of Christ—much like the tools used to shape and form pottery.

In other words, the Word of God is formational. Like a scalpel in the hand of a skilled doctor, God's Word shapes and develops our worship. As we spend time with Him in His Word, our worship is shaped by what we read. The Holy Spirit enables us to worship more deeply. And in the process our lives, relationships, ministries, and evangelism are shaped by that worship.

SCRIPTURE SHAPES OUR DOCTRINE

A primary reason God's Word is formational is that it shapes our core beliefs about the most important elements of life. It shapes our theology, for example. Theology is the study of God, so it's hard to imagine a more important subject. What we believe about God influences what we believe about everything else.

Scripture shapes our beliefs about God. In addition to our personal experiences with Him, what we know of God is based on what He's revealed about Himself through His Word. Therefore, as we spend time worshiping God and studying His truth, we learn more about Him. He uses His Word to form our belief system—our doctrine. And as we understand doctrine, God speaks to our hearts about how we should apply biblical truth to daily living.

How does this process play out in our routine of worship and evangelism? Let's say you learn from the Bible that God wants all people from all nations to worship Him and that salvation is available to all people groups in the world. Based on that knowledge, you conclude that all people need to be worshipers of the Most High God. And based on your belief, you develop a personal strategy for telling people how to become disciples and worshipers of God. Finally, you obey what God has shown you by sharing the gospel at every opportunity He provides.

What are some other truths you've learned about God from the Bible? Record three.

1.

2.

3.

What are some implications of those truths for your everyday life?

A CASE STUDY

Josiah's story from the Book of 2 Kings powerfully illustrates the formational quality of God's Word. Although Josiah was anointed king of Judah at the tender age of 8, he recognized that his father and many other prior kings had led the nation of Judah in rebellion against God.

Josiah did the best he could to turn the kingdom away from wickedness, but he lacked guidance. He didn't know how to properly glorify God. Then something changed as his servants worked to repair the temple: "Shaphan the court secretary told the king, 'Hilkiah the priest has given me a book,' and Shaphan read it in the presence of the king" (2 Kings 22:10).

The book Shaphan read was the law God had given to Moses—probably the Book of Deuteronomy or perhaps the entire Pentateuch (the first five books of the Old Testament). In any case Josiah was exposed to God's Word for the first time in his young life, and it changed him. He was instantly aware of the many ways the people of Judah had rebelled against God. He was so stricken with grief that he tore his clothes and pleaded for God's forgiveness. He commanded the people to tear down idols and false gods in the nation. For the first time in decades, he led the people in observing the feast of Passover, as God's Word commanded.

Read 2 Kings 22:8-13. When have you been convicted of wrongdoing by something you read in God's Word? What happened next?

Read 2 Kings 22:14-20. How was Josiah's life changed because of his response to God's Word?

What changes would you like God to make in you as you interact with His Word?

There's a vital cause-and-effect relationship at play between our exposure to God's Word and our formation as His followers. And this relationship is essential to the process of Great Commission worship.

Our study of God's Word shapes our worship and what we believe. The more the Holy Spirit changes our belief system, the more we want to know the Bible. The more time we spend reading the Bible, the more we want to know about God. The more we understand about God, the more we want to worship. This process goes on and on. In the end this cycle plays an important role in our growth as Great Commission worshipers and followers of God.

TODAY'S EVANGELISM EXPRESSION

Take a moment to record some of the main ways your life has changed since you relinquished control and began to follow Jesus.
• What do you value most in life? Why?
• What are your current goals, and how do you plan to accomplish them?
• How do you find happiness, purpose, and satisfaction?
• How have your answers to these questions changed since you first encountered Jesus?

TODAY'S WORSHIP EXPRESSION

In many ways Psalm 119 is a love poem written with God's Word as the subject. Take a few minutes to read the psalm on your own. Try reading out loud if you would find it meaningful to hear the imagery and cadence of the language. Meditate on the different ways you also appreciate the Scriptures. Afterward express that appreciation to God through prayer.

DAY 5

GO AND MAKE DISCIPLES

If you've ever reared kids or been around kids for any significant period of time, you've probably noticed that they can have a hard time discerning between suggestions and commands, usually depending on their moods and interests.

"I might like some ice cream tonight" can sound like a noncommittal statement, but your children may hear it as a firm decision and immediately jump to the kitchen table with spoons in hand. On the other hand, if you tell your kids, "Go and clean your room before you play with your friends," they may receive your words as a mere suggestion and make their own decision about whether to obey.

That kind of behavior is mildly frustrating when displayed by children, but it's damning when otherwise mature followers of Jesus decide to treat lightly what He's clearly commanded us to do.

Look again at the Great Commission, for example:

> Jesus came near and said to them, "All authority has been given to Me in heaven and on earth. Go, therefore, and make disciples of all nations, baptizing them in the name of the Father and of the Son and of the Holy Spirit, teaching them to observe everything I have commanded you. And remember, I am with you always, to the end of the age."
>
> Matthew 28:18-20

What commands are included in those verses?

How have those commands impacted your everyday life?

What are some other scriptural commands that Christians don't always take seriously?

Today we'll take a deeper look at Jesus' command to "make disciples of all nations" (v. 19) and explore why it's an essential part of Great Commission worship.

A MANDATE FOR ALL OF US

After His resurrection Jesus spent several days appearing to different people and teaching His followers many things. But He didn't stay for long. Soon Jesus gathered His followers on the Mount of Olives before ascending into heaven:

> When they had come together, they asked Him, "Lord, are You restoring the kingdom to Israel at this time?" He said to them, "It is not for you to know times or periods that the Father has set by His own authority. But you will receive power when the Holy Spirit has come on you, and you will be My witnesses in Jerusalem, in all Judea and Samaria, and to the ends of the earth."
>
> Acts 1:6-8

The contrast between the disciples' question and Jesus' statement is intriguing. They asked whether He was about to restore the nation of Israel to its former glory, overthrowing the Roman Empire in the process. Even after all they'd seen and heard, they were still clinging to the old dream of an earthly kingdom.

Jesus' answer was firm: "It is not for you to know" (v. 7). In other words, it wasn't an idea the disciples needed to spend a lot of time or energy thinking about. Jesus continued with what they *did* need to concentrate on: "But you will receive power … and you will be My witnesses" (v. 8). Notice the certainty in Jesus' words: "You *will*." There was no question about whether the disciples would participate in evangelism. Jesus gave them a mandate, and He fully expected them to obey. He fully expects us to obey as well.

Read the following passages of Scripture and record what they teach about our mandate to make disciples.

Matthew 5:13-16

Romans 10:14-15

1 Peter 3:13-17

What emotions do you experience when you read these verses? Why?

Look again at Acts 1:8, especially the last phrase: "You will receive power when the Holy Spirit has come on you, and you will be My witnesses in Jerusalem, in all Judea and Samaria, and *to the ends of the earth*" (emphasis added). We may be tempted to believe Jesus was speaking only to the disciples. After all, they were the ones who carried the gospel throughout Jerusalem and Judea.

But the last phrase refuses to let us off the hook: "and to the ends of the earth." That's our responsibility. That's been one of the primary missions of the church for the past two thousand years, and it reminds us of our primary mission today. There are still places where the gospel hasn't been proclaimed, still people who haven't heard the good news. This is true of the ends of the earth, but it's also true of our own towns and neighborhoods. Maybe our own homes.

Think of the people you regularly interact with who haven't experienced the salvation offered by Jesus. Record three names.

1.

2.

3.

A PART OF OUR FORMATION

As Great Commission worshipers, we've been commanded to share the good news of the gospel with those who need to hear it. That's part of what it means to be a Christian. Our obedience in this area brings glory to God whether or not our evangelistic efforts produce fruit.

We also need to understand that just as worship is a key element in our spiritual formation, evangelism plays a major role in shaping us to become more like Christ. Evangelism is formational.

We get a clear picture of this concept from the natural world. In nature a key characteristic shared by all living organisms is their ability to reproduce. The potential to produce new life is a sign of health and vitality, and organisms aren't considered fully developed without it.

In a similar way, seeking to produce new life on a spiritual level is an important milestone in our development as followers of Jesus. We demonstrate spiritual maturity when we evangelize, and the process of sharing our faith ultimately increases that maturity.

The life of Peter is a great illustration of these truths.

Read Acts 2:14-39. What do you find most surprising or interesting in these verses? Why?

What words in the text describe Peter's actions?

Peter accompanied Jesus for most of His public ministry, and he'd learned much as a disciple. But that knowledge hadn't always resulted in wisdom and correct actions. Indeed, Peter was known more for putting his foot in his mouth than for spiritual growth and maturity, a trend that culminated when he publicly denied Jesus three times before the crucifixion (see Matt. 26:69-75).

Things changed after Jesus' ascension, however, and after Peter received the Holy Spirit on the day of Pentecost. In Acts 2 Peter's bold proclamation of the gospel revealed his newfound maturity as a follower of Jesus. His efforts contributed to the spiritual rebirth of thousands of people (see v. 41), and the experience further matured Peter as he grew into a major leader in the early church.

The same process can work for us. Indeed, it must if we're to successfully glorify God as Great Commission worshipers.

Think of the lost people you named earlier today. How do you think you would grow as a Christian if you began to share your faith with them regularly?

TODAY'S EVANGELISM EXPRESSION

Conclude this week of study by preparing a written testimony of your faith in Jesus Christ and the many ways that faith has impacted your life.

If that sounds daunting, don't worry. You've been preparing for this assignment all week by answering the questions in Today's Evangelism Expression at the end of each day. Looking over your answers to those questions will give you a clear progression of your life before Christ, your encounters with Him and with the truth of the gospel, and how you've been changed as a result.

Your assignment for today is to compile those answers into a written testimony of faith. Using whatever form of writing you're most comfortable with—paragraphs, a bullet list, a flowchart, and so on—record your story in a way that will allow you to express it clearly and concisely whenever you have an opportunity to share it.

TODAY'S WORSHIP EXPRESSION

As you worship in your local church this week, bring to the service a reminder of your old life before you encountered Christ. This could be an old item of clothing, a piece of jewelry, a DVD, a song—anything that represents the life from which Jesus rescued you. Concentrate on that item as you participate in the service. Allow yourself to remember what it was like to be lost. Respond with praise and gratitude because Christ found you and saved you.

1. Westminster Shorter Catechism [online, cited 6 September 2012]. Available from the Internet: www.reformed.org/documents/WSC.html.
2. Sermon Illustrations [online, cited 7 September 2012]. Available from the Internet: www.sermonillustrations.com.

WEEK 1 GROUP EXPERIENCE

Use the following activity to introduce the topics covered in this week's study.

SUPPLIES NEEDED. Two slices of bread for each participant, one jar of peanut butter, one jar of jelly, knives, napkins, and paper plates

ACTIVITY. To introduce the themes in this study and to facilitate introductions between participants, make peanut-butter-and-jelly sandwiches. As you work on the sandwiches, discuss the following questions.

What else goes together like peanut butter and jelly? Answers can include people, images, ideas, and so on.

How do worship and evangelism complement each other?

What did you like best about the material in week 1? Why?

What questions would you like to discuss as a group?

Prepare for further group discussion by reading aloud the following passages.

> He said to him, " 'Love the Lord your God with all your
> heart, with all your soul, and with all your mind.' This is
> the greatest and most important command. The second
> is like it: 'Love your neighbor as yourself.' All the Law
> and the Prophets depend on these two commands."
>
> Matthew 22:37-40

> Go, therefore, and make disciples of all nations,
> baptizing them in the name of the Father and of the
> Son and of the Holy Spirit, teaching them to observe
> everything I have commanded you. And remember,
> I am with you always, to the end of the age.
>
> Matthew 28:19-20

Use the following excerpts from the study material to move below the surface and engage in transformational conversations.

DAY 1. The reason we often perceive a separation between worship and evangelism is that many Christians and many churches possess a false view of each experience. There's a disconnect between the biblical view of worship and evangelism and the way we often carry out those activities.

For example, many Christians' conceptions of worship are limited to an emotional high on Sunday mornings, yet during the week they ignore Jesus' mandate to go and make disciples of all nations. At the same time, many Christians feel pressure to try and "bring people to Jesus." But without grounding their efforts in genuine worship, they win converts but fail to make disciples who are true worshipers.

Jesus' words in the Great Commandment (see Matt. 22:37-40) and the Great Commission (see Matt. 28:19-20) express the heart of both worship and evangelism. He called us to glorify God with unyielding allegiance, but our worship isn't complete unless we also love our neighbor. If we fall in love with Christ and seek to glorify His name, we'll also love others and lead them to worship with us.

Neither evangelism nor worship is an isolated religious activity; both combine to form a lifestyle that seeks to glorify God by joining Him on mission every day. Jesus calls us to Great Commission worship.

During what seasons of life have you had passionate, meaningful experiences of worshiping God?

During what seasons of life have you been motivated and successful in sharing your faith?

DAY 2. Great Commission worship is formational. It sculpts us and shapes us into something new. The more we glorify God through worship and evangelism, the more we're conformed to His image. This happens every time we feast on God's Word, worship the God of the Word, apply His Word to our lives, share the gospel with a friend, and experience God's mercies new every morning.

How has your spiritual growth been impacted by worship?

How has your spiritual growth been impacted by evangelism?

DAY 3. This week we're focusing on the fact that genuine experiences with Great Commission worship are formational: they sculpt and shape us into something new. Here's the best news: the something new we're being shaped into is actually Jesus. As we worship God and share our faith, we're molded more and more into the image of Christ.

Great Commission worship is the proper response to who Jesus is and everything He's done on our behalf. No other message is more important for us to share, and no other person is more worthy of our praise.

In your own words, how would you define Great Commission worship?

In what ways are you more like Jesus today than when you first encountered Him?

DAY 4. The Word of God is formational. Like a scalpel in the hand of a skilled doctor, God's Word shapes and develops our worship. As we spend time with Him in His Word, our worship is shaped by what we read. The Holy Spirit enables us to worship more deeply. And in the process our lives, relationships, ministries, and evangelism are shaped by that worship.

Read 2 Kings 22:8-13. When have you been convicted of wrongdoing by something you read in God's Word? What happened next?

Read 2 Kings 22:14-20. How was Josiah's life changed because of his response to God's Word?

What changes would you like God to make in you as you interact with His Word?

DAY 5. As Great Commission worshipers, we've been commanded to share the good news of the gospel with those who need to hear it. That's part of what it means to be a Christian. Our obedience in this area brings glory to God whether or not our evangelistic efforts produce fruit. But we also need to understand that just as worship is a key element in our spiritual formation, evangelism also plays a major role in shaping us to become more like Christ. Evangelism is formational.

Read the following passages of Scripture and discuss what they teach about our mandate to make disciples.

Matthew 5:13-16

Romans 10:14-15

1 Peter 3:13-17

What emotions do you experience when you read these verses? Why?

APPLY TO LIFE

Discuss your experiences with the Evangelism Expression and Worship Expression at the end of each day's study material.

What emotions did you experience while preparing your written testimony this week?

If you're willing and as time allows, share your testimonies of coming to faith in Jesus Christ.

The Worship Expression in day 5 included this challenge: "As you worship in your local church this week, bring to the service a reminder of your old life before you encountered Christ." What item did you choose? Why?

PRAY

As you conclude this group session, pray that God will grant you opportunities to share your testimony in the coming weeks. Also pray that the Holy Spirit will regularly remind you to focus on worshiping God throughout each day.

GREAT COMMISSION WORSHIP IS TRANSFORMATIONAL

Although physics is an important field of study, not many people would claim it as their favorite subject in school.

All of those theories and equations can be overwhelming. But there are a few laws from the world of physics that most find easy to understand. Like Sir Issac Newton's laws of motion.

Newton's first law states that an object at rest will stay at rest unless acted on by an outside force. Also, an object in motion will stay in motion until something throws it off course. These are pretty simple concepts. An object can't change the state it's in unless something or someone interacts with it.

In the same way, believers can be objects at rest, inactive and stagnant in our Christian lives. Although God intended for us to grow into the likeness of His Son, Jesus, it's possible for us to fail to grow spiritually. However, once we begin to connect with the power of the Holy Spirit, He stimulates growth and brings about transformation in our lives.

Great Commission worship is transformational. God, through the Holy Spirit, is in the business of changing people. The power of the Holy Spirit changes broken, sinful people into worshipers of the living God. He transforms lives from hurting and broken to healed and re-created. As He transforms us into the likeness of Jesus, we're equipped to teach, train, encourage, edify, and share the gospel with the lost so that they can become Great Commission worshipers of the living God.

DAY 1

WORSHIP AND OBEDIENCE

People are generally afraid of change. And the older you get, the more this statement is true. The popular phrase is "If it ain't broke, don't fix it." The problem is that we're all desperately broken. In our attempts to change, we make resolutions and promises we often can't keep. In many ways we try to fix ourselves, but to no avail. Only the power of the Holy Spirit in our lives can thrust us toward real transformation and Great Commission worship.

What resolutions or promises have you made that you haven't been able to keep?

In your own words, what is transformation?

A NEW NATURE

If you're a child of God, you experienced the work of the Holy Spirit at salvation. This was so much more than renovation. It was more than simply taking something dirty and cleaning it up to make it pretty. Your regeneration was a total change of your very nature from the inside out. Paul described it this way: "If anyone is in Christ, he is a new creation; old things have passed away, and look, new things have come" (2 Cor. 5:17).

What did Paul mean by "old things" and "new things"?

How did the Holy Spirit change you at the moment of your salvation?

Paul said the old is gone, completely replaced by the new. The Holy Spirit hasn't merely reshaped or renovated what was corrupted by sin. The corrupted is gone, making room for an entirely new creation with an entirely new nature. Now Christ is living in you.

In the same way the Holy Spirit works at regeneration, He continues to work in you to transform you into the likeness of Jesus. Although you're a new creation in Christ, the Spirit still takes you through a process of embracing and living out the character of Jesus. Paul explained it this way: "You have put off the old self with its practices and have put on the new self. You are being renewed in knowledge according to the image of your Creator" (Col. 3:9-10).

Did you get that? You've already put off the old self, yet you're being renewed. Transformation is an ongoing, lifelong process. And it can be accomplished only by the Holy Spirit.

When our hearts remain attentive to the Spirit's transformational work, we can experience transformational worship and display the Spirit's work to the world:

> As it is written:
> What eye did not see and ear did not hear,
> and what never entered the human mind—
> God prepared this for those who love Him.
>
> Now God has revealed these things to us by the Spirit, for the Spirit searches everything, even the depths of God. For who among men knows the thoughts of a man except the spirit of the man that is in him? In the same way, no one knows the thoughts of God except the Spirit of God. Now we have not received the spirit of the world, but the Spirit who comes from God, so that we may understand what has been freely given to us by God. We also speak these things, not in words taught by human wisdom, but in those taught by the Spirit, explaining spiritual things to spiritual people.
>
> 1 Corinthians 2:9-13

What does this passage reveal about the role of the Holy Spirit in transformation?

In what ways have you experienced Spirit-empowered transformation in your life?

When we're transformed into Christlikeness, our expressions of worship and evangelism are changed. As we go into the world to fulfill the Great Commission and as we exalt God, we long to see others become Great Commission worshipers as well. At the same time, our experiences of witnessing and worship are themselves transformational. The Holy Spirit changes our hearts as we obey Jesus' call to fulfill the Great Commission and the Great Commandment.

OBEDIENCE IS AT THE CORE

One way we experience transformation is through obedience to the Holy Spirit's direction. Read this promise about God's work through His Spirit:

> I will give you a new heart and put a new spirit within you;
> I will remove your heart of stone and give you a heart of
> flesh. I will place My Spirit within you and cause you to
> follow My statutes and carefully observe My ordinances.
>
> Ezekiel 36:26-27

What do these verses teach you about obedience?

How do these verses say obedience is carried out?

Obedience is at the core of authentic, transformational worship and evangelism. We demonstrate our love—our worship—of God best when we do what He tells us to do. When we obey His Word, our worship becomes transformational.

What are some specific ways you've seen your obedience
to God transform your life?

What happens when our obedience is directed toward ritual
instead of toward genuine worship?

God desires hearts of obedience. It's not the details of worship that transform our lives. It's not the worship songs we sing, the prayers we pray, the sermons we deliver, the engaging and moving videos about missions we watch, the offerings we bring, the invitations we give, or the testimonies we share that transform our lives. Transformation comes only when the Lord receives our songs, prayers, sermons, offerings, testimonies, service, and obedience as sincere, honest, personal gifts of love for Him—and to Him. If the ceremony of worship transformed our lives, worship would become mere ritual. The Holy Spirit—not our actions, service, or formal procedure for worship—transforms our lives.

Actually, our acts of worship don't do anything to change us. It's during worship that the Holy Spirit begins to break down the bitterness, anger, self-promoting attitudes, and greed in our hearts. And it's this kind of transformation that changes a life, family, church, and nation.

How have you experienced spiritual transformation through worship?

Through witnessing?

AN OBEDIENT PROPHET

Isaiah was a prophet to Judah, the southern kingdom of Israel, before its exile to Babylon. He was a man of great vision and forthrightness about the events of his time, the imminent captivity of Judah, and the coming of Jesus Christ as King of kings. After the Assyrians had devastated the northern kingdom, Isaiah prophesied against the Assyrian king and spoke with conviction about the arrogance displayed by that ungodly, vile nation (see Isa. 10:5-34).

Isaiah foretold that God was going to carry out His purposes through the Messiah. During the reigns of Uzziah; Jotham; Ahaz, a wicked, idolatrous monarch; and Hezekiah, a godly man who sought to remove idolatry from the land, Isaiah proclaimed the truth about the Messiah who would establish His kingdom over the whole earth.

Read Isaiah 6:1-10. At this point in Isaiah's journey, worship became a very personal experience. What are some points that stand out to you in this passage?

In this passage we witness seven steps to transformational worship in the life of Isaiah.

1. Isaiah recognized God sitting on a very high throne, and God allowed Isaiah to see His glory (see vv. 1-4). This one experience gave Isaiah enough power to do the work of God for the rest of his life. Like Abraham, Jacob, Moses, Joshua, Samuel, Deborah, and Gideon before, the prophet was never the same after witnessing the sheer magnitude of God's glory.

2. Isaiah was struck with a spirit of conviction (see v. 5a). He perceived his own sinfulness. His response was personal. He didn't send a surrogate to God. Rather, he personally sought God with passion. He wanted to do something about his helpless condition, no matter the cost. Instinctively, he knew the first step was repentance.

3. Isaiah professed his faith by confessing his sin (see v. 5b). He understood the depth of his sin, and he understood the consequences of being in the company of sinners. He took a hard look at himself and in essence said, "God, I'm not worthy to be in Your presence. I'm a sinner" (authors' paraphrase).

4. Isaiah sought forgiveness and cleansing (see vv. 6-7). Once he confessed his need for forgiveness, God took over. Cleansing, purifying, and purging of sin were all God. So it is with you and me. God is the One responsible for cleaning us up: "You are saved by grace through faith, and this is not from yourselves; it is God's gift—not from works, so that no one can boast" (Eph. 2:8-9). We only need to confess our need and submit to His authority. He does the rest.

5. Isaiah heard God's call (see Isa. 6:8a). He heard God's voice, perceived the need, and recognized a calling from God. God's call isn't for the faint of heart. He didn't tell Isaiah the task, duty, or job would be easy. He gave Isaiah the responsibility of proclaiming judgment and blessing, justice and righteousness, punishment and hope, devastation and salvation. No other prophet had ever been given such a daunting task.

6. Isaiah answered God's call (see v. 8b). Isaiah gave God total dedication and devotion. He made a pledge to God and consecrated his confession by responding, "Here I am. Send me."

7. Isaiah received his commission and charge (see vv. 9-10). He captured a sense of his task and immediately obeyed. The job wasn't going to be easy, but Isaiah received his instructions, accepted his duty, and served the Lord with passion.

What did you learn from Isaiah about obedience as an element of Great Commission worship?

Obedience comes from a heart of worship. And God enriches our worship as we obey His voice. Obedience to God's Word is foundational to worshiping God.

Isaiah teaches us that worship of God is at the core of our response to salvation through Christ. Worship isn't determined by our faithfulness to the law. Our worship is evidenced or confirmed by our love for God.

TODAY'S EVANGELISM EXPRESSION

Think about a time when you needed the transforming work of God to come into your life when you felt powerless. Answer the following questions.
• How did you attempt to change on your own? What happened?
• How did you finally come to grips with your weakness?
• Are you experiencing that same kind of powerlessness right now? How are you allowing the Holy Spirit to work?

TODAY'S WORSHIP EXPRESSION

Read Ezekiel 36:26-27 again and reflect on how God is at work in your heart. Praise Him for His transforming power through the Spirit. Express your need for forgiveness and cleansing and allow God to do the rest. Ask Him to show you areas in your life in which you need to rely on Him to be obedient.

DAY 2

WORSHIP AND REPENTANCE

"You're special." "Someday we'll be watching you on *Monday Night Football*." "If you keep your head on straight, you'll go pro and make millions." Talented young athletes often hear phrases like these. And they're indeed true for many who aspire to be successful at a sport in which they excel. They find success in their particular sport; they make their millions; and when their sports career is over, they live comfortably for the rest of their lives. But for others with equal or greater talent, it's not as easy.

If you pay any attention to professional sports, you've probably noticed a trend among some of the more troubled athletes. Poor attitudes, moral failures, or drug abuse plagues them throughout careers that are often short and disappointing. Despite the warnings from coaches, family, and mentors and the risk of losing everything they've worked for, they continue on a path of destruction, wasting their incredible talent.

From the outside looking in, we want to say, "Wake up! What are you thinking? Learn from your mistakes and help my team win!"

But don't we often find ourselves saying the same thing about our own sin or the sins of the ones we love? Just like the continuing moral failures of athletes, sin has a way of lingering. Attaching itself to us like a leech, it robs us of our ability to be Great Commission worshipers.

Read James 1:14-15. Describe the progression of sin these verses present. What do these verses say about the seriousness of sin?

How do we become aware of sin in our lives?

What actions should we take when we become aware of our sin?

What comes to mind when you hear the word repentance? Why?

We started this week by discussing the role obedience plays in Great Commission worship. Today let's focus on the effects of sin and the way worship leads us to an awareness of our sin. Once we realize the ugliness and severity of our sin in comparison to our awesome Lord, our first act of worship is to seek forgiveness and restoration with God. Then we recognize Him as the King of kings and Lord of lords. As we repent, God transforms us and makes us new.

AN UNPOPULAR TERM

The word *repentance* isn't the most glamorous term in Christian vocabulary. It normally conjures up two feelings.

First, this term presumes something is wrong with us, something that prevents us from experiencing genuine worship and from making disciples. Our pride hates this feeling and does everything in its power to fight against this admission. Second, we consider repentance to be hard work because it requires removing a desire or a practice in our lives that temporarily gives us pleasure.

Bob Deffinbaugh gives us an additional perspective:

> Repentance is not a very "in" word, and certainly not a very popular practice. It begins, I believe, with a renewed grasp of the holiness of God, and thus a realization of the immensity of our sin. It leads to a whole new way of looking at life, this time through God's eyes, as conveyed through the Holy Scriptures. *It is a revulsion toward sin, so that we determine not to repeat it. It results in a renewed sense of God's presence, a new joy in our salvation, and a desire to turn others from sin.*[1]

When we worship, we become aware of the presence and immensity of our sin. We get a glimpse of the way God views our sin, causing us to seek repentance.

How have you recently become aware of a particular sin in your life?

How does sin affect your ability to experience genuine worship?

What does sin do to your effectiveness as a witness?

Describe a time when you experienced true repentance.
Was it difficult? Explain.

A PICTURE OF REPENTANCE

Scripture gives several examples of repentance. One that stands out is found in 2 Samuel 11–12, the account of David's adultery with Bathsheba. This passage provides a humbling look at the way our sins affect our relationships with those around us and with God. But through David's sin and its consequences, we also get a glimpse of God's grace, love, and forgiveness. All of these factors eventually pointed David toward true repentance.

Read 2 Samuel 11:1-17. List some of the sins David committed.

Why does a single sin often lead to other sins? How have you seen this happen in your life?

Although David was a man after God's heart (see 1 Sam. 13:14), he was still a fallen creature, subject to temptation and sin. When David attempted to cover up his sin, it only made things worse and led to consequence after consequence. But when the bottom dropped out and he came face-to-face with his sin and its effects, he could still experience God's transformative power.

This painful experience brought David to a point of genuine repentance for his sin, followed by forgiveness and restoration from God. The same thing happens when we recognize and confess our guilt.

Read 2 Samuel 11:26–12:15. Who has been a "Nathan" who's led you to an awareness of your sin? For whom has God called you to be a "Nathan"?

Nathan's parable allowed David to see his sin and move toward confession and repentance. David described this process in Psalm 51:2-4:

> Wash away my guilt
> and cleanse me from my sin.
> For I am conscious of my rebellion,
> and my sin is always before me.
> Against You—You alone—I have sinned
> and done this evil in Your sight.
> So You are right when You pass sentence;
> You are blameless when You judge.

How are we transformed when we acknowledge our sins and seek forgiveness?

How does repentance affect our relationship with God?

Practically, how can we develop better habits of confession?

Like David, we need to confess our sins to God, admitting that we've rebelled against Him and acknowledging that His ways are righteous and holy. Confession also leads us to worship when we experience His mercy and cleansing power.

What behavior in your life contradicts God's expectations? What effect does this behavior have on your witness in the world?

Read 2 Samuel 12:16-25. What's significant about David's response when his son died? What does this tell you about the current condition of his relationship with God?

Death came to their son, but God's grace began anew in the lives of David and Bathsheba. Later Solomon was born and would become the next king of Israel.

David's story points us to the cross. If you're a believer, you've acknowledged that death is also the consequence of your sins. But in His mercy God substituted the death of another as the payment for those sins:

> When you were slaves of sin, you were free from allegiance to righteousness. So what fruit was produced then from the things you are now ashamed of? For the end of those things is death. But now, since you have been liberated from sin and have become enslaved to God, you have your fruit, which results in sanctification—and the end is eternal life! For the wages of sin is death, but the gift of God is eternal life in Christ Jesus our Lord.
>
> Romans 6:20-23

How is it possible for God to use people to serve Him even after they've sinned?

How have you seen God offer you mercy and grace after you sinned?

Even after we surrender our lives to Christ, we still struggle with sin, but in His mercy God uses a number of ways to lead us to repentance. God makes us aware of our sin through the Holy Spirit's conviction, His Word, a "Nathan," a church gathering, and many other ways. Regardless of how we see His hand of mercy, we should acknowledge our sin and our need of a Savior and renew our relationship with God through a process of repentance. This may be a difficult and daunting undertaking, but repentance offers a significant means of spiritual growth for those who submit to the Holy Spirit's leadership in this process.

Although we're sinful people who deserve death and hell, because of the cross God forgives us. We're made righteous in His eyes because we've been justified by His grace. In response we're called to live in a continual attitude of worship and in total submission to the King, ready and willing to tell others about our experience.

TODAY'S EVANGELISM EXPRESSION

It's important to remind yourself of ways God has acted in your life to restore you to Himself. Reflect on a time when you became aware of your sin and went through a process of repentance.
- How did God bring you to an awareness of your sin?
- How did you experience the Holy Spirit's transforming power?
- Was the process of repentance difficult? Explain.
- How can your experience give you the means and credibility to be a "Nathan" to someone else?

TODAY'S WORSHIP EXPRESSION

Ask God to make you aware of your sin through the Holy Spirit. Take a few moments to reflect on the cross and to thank Jesus for dying the death you deserved. Think about how much you deserve death and hell and how desperately you need His saving power.

DAY 3

WORSHIP AND SPIRITUAL GROWTH

It's common to feel inadequate when we compare ourselves to heroes of the faith. And not just to guys like Paul, Moses, and Peter but even when lined up against our own pastor, mentor, or spouse. All of these people might make us question if we'll ever reach their level of spiritual maturity.

There are two problems with this thinking.

1. We're not allowing ourselves to trust in the transforming power of God.

2. Second, we haven't taken a step back to see the road taken by the one to whom we're comparing ourselves. We haven't seen their spiritual victories; their trials; or their methodical, step-by-step progression toward faithfulness.

No one suddenly arrives at spiritual maturity. And it can't be accomplished alone.

God is glorified when He sees His work grow and develop in our lives. It's God who gives comfort, peace, contentment, and direction for life. As we worship and tell others about Him, we experience His comfort, His peace, and His love in powerful ways. And He gives us opportunities to walk with Him, talk with Him, trust Him, and declare His wonders to unbelievers around us.

In other words, God transforms our daily walk.

Describe what an ideal daily walk with God looks like.

Which of these elements are already present in your walk?
Which need to be added?

REQUIREMENTS FOR SPIRITUAL GROWTH

Scripture shows us the relationship between spiritual growth and transformation. It also gives us an inside look at how transformation takes place:

> We all, with unveiled faces, are looking as in a mirror at the glory of the Lord and are being transformed into the same image from glory to glory; this is from the Lord who is the Spirit.
>
> 2 Corinthians 3:18

Robertson McQuilkin points out two qualifications for spiritual transformation.

1. First, in the verses leading up to verse 18, Paul explained that the Jews read Scripture but couldn't understand it because of sin barriers in their lives. Their faces, minds, and hearts were veiled. But when they turned to God with "unveiled faces" and their sin barrier was removed, they were able to worship God and grow toward spiritual maturity.

2. We're transformed when we focus on God's glory as intently as we would gaze into a mirror. McQuilkin uses Hebrews 12:1-2 to help us understand and maintain this kind of focus:[2]

   > Since we also have such a large cloud of witnesses surrounding us, let us lay aside every weight and the sin that so easily ensnares us. Let us run with endurance the race that lies before us, keeping our eyes on Jesus, the source and perfecter of our faith, who for the joy that lay before Him endured a cross and despised the shame and has sat down at the right hand of God's throne.

Based on this passage, how would you describe a life that keeps a steady focus on Jesus?

To what extent does your life exhibit these characteristics?

McQuilkin concludes, "Unveiled-face people and focused-on-Jesus people are the ones who experience a steady transformation at the core of their beings."[3] Once we have the sin barrier removed, focus our worship on "the source and perfecter of our faith" (v. 2), and share this truth with others, we begin to experience transformation. We experience what it means to be Great Commission worshipers.

AN ENCOUNTER WITH GOD

Scripture offers several examples of this kind of spiritual growth. But maybe the most noteworthy example is Moses.

At the time of Moses' birth, the children of Israel were in slavery. Pharaoh, being concerned about a revolt because of the increasing population of the Israelites, ordered the execution of all male children born to Israelites. Moses' mother hid him for three months but was ultimately forced to send him down the Nile River in a basket, hoping someone would find, protect, and raise him. Pharaoh's daughter found Moses and raised him in Pharaoh's home.

When Moses was grown, he began to see and vocalize his frustration with the injustice carried out by the Egyptians against the Israelite people. This frustration led him to kill an Egyptian who was beating a fellow Hebrew. In fear for his life, Moses fled to the land of Midian, where he became a shepherd for 40 years.

That's when Moses encountered God. Leading his flock in the wilderness, Moses came upon a burning bush from which the voice of God spoke. If this image wasn't disconcerting enough, God told Moses that he would be the one to lead God's people out of captivity. Immediately intimidated and frightened, Moses questioned God and doubted His ability to use him: "Who am I that I should go to Pharaoh and that I should bring the Israelites out of Egypt?" (Ex. 3:11).

Read Exodus 3:14-15. How did God respond to Moses' doubt? What was significant about His response?

Describe a time when you doubted God's ability to use you. Was your doubt primarily directed toward God or toward yourself?

How does our trust in God affect our ability to grow spiritually?

God gave Moses many miraculous signs to show the Israelites. He also gave him the reassurance that He would be with him, but Moses continued to doubt his ability to carry out this task.

The truth is, this task indeed appeared impossible from the start. How could Moses, by himself, carry out such an enormous assignment? He couldn't. He needed supernatural help. And as we'll find out, once Moses had confidence in God's presence and power, he was able to be an instrumental part of an event that would forever change the course of Jewish history.

What assignment has God recently called you to do that you fear you can't handle on your own?

What promises and truths from Scripture has God provided to help you confront that fear?

What spiritual growth has come about in your life because God showed Himself to you in a powerful way? What did He show you?

Moses finally obeyed and sought the freedom of his people. But Pharaoh wouldn't give up without a fight. Why would he? What authority and power could one man have over Pharaoh? Yet Scripture tells us that 10 plagues later, Pharaoh released the Israelites to Moses. God demonstrated His absolute authority, and they were on their way out of Egypt. But then Pharaoh had a change of heart.

Read Exodus 14:5-14. How did Moses' reaction to the Israelites' fear reveal his spiritual growth since the time of the burning bush?

The Israelites were trapped and perceived death as inevitable and unavoidable, despite Moses' encouragement of the Lord's provision. But in one of the most marvelous displays of divine power in human history, God revealed Himself to the Israelites at the Red Sea.

Read Exodus 14:21-31. What role did Moses play in God's deliverance of the Hebrew people?

Has God given you the opportunity to tell of His provision and salvation? How did you respond?

From Moses' initial fear at the burning bush to his role in God's deliverance, Moses displayed significant spiritual growth. At first doubtful and afraid, he was later able to trust God and step out in obedience to become useful in God's plan. This step of faith allowed God to develop in Moses the courage and strength of character he needed to stand up to a tyrant and lead a nation out of bondage.

Spiritual growth may not always be an easy process, but when we submit ourselves to God's work in our lives, we place ourselves in a position for Him to change us and use us for His glory.

TODAY'S EVANGELISM EXPRESSION

Record some ways you've seen spiritual transformation in your life.
- What's your burning-bush experience?
- How has God transformed your worship and perception of Him since that experience?
- Who in your life needs to hear about this? Think about people in your life for whom your experience could be meaningful. Write their names beside your notes on life transformation.

TODAY'S WORSHIP EXPRESSION

We all have doubts at some level. But transformational worship is about trusting God with those doubts. He doesn't expect or desire for us to carry that kind of burden. Spend time today meditating on God's presence in your life and in your experiences. Thank Him for allowing you to depend on Him and for helping you grow in the likeness of Jesus through the challenging times of life.

DAY 4

WORSHIP AND RELATIONSHIP

"I take you to be my lawfully wedded wife, to have and to hold, from this day forward, for better, for worse, for richer, for poorer, in sickness and in health, to love and to cherish till death do us part. And hereto I pledge you my faithfulness."

These are words a man might say to a woman during a marriage ceremony, and she'd reciprocate with a similar vow. However, the value of these words should be far greater than a marriage certificate. When you enter a commitment to a genuine love relationship, you make a promise and pledge of loyalty, faithfulness, and steadfastness, no matter what circumstances may arise. It's not the same as scrolling to the end of an electronic document to click on the "I accept" button.

"Till death do us part." Those are powerful words of commitment with profound implications. But sometimes that's all they are: just words. There's no sincerity or commitment behind them.

What commitments have you made to God? Did these come from a genuine heart of worship, or were they more legalistic in nature?

When do you find yourself going through the motions as a follower of Jesus?

A bride's and a groom's vows point beyond the words to a deep, committed love relationship. Similarly, God isn't as concerned with the words of our vows or acts of our worship as He is with the motivation and commitment behind our words and actions. He wants deeply committed worshipers, not cookie-cutter Christians who say the right words and do the right things at the right times.

God created us to worship as an expression of His plan for our lives—to know Him. And because He greatly desires an active, personal relationship with His children, He's provided an avenue for communication with Him. But He's also given us a hunger for completeness in Him and has provided a way for us to grow in our love relationship with Him. This is transformational worship.

AN INTIMATE LOVE RELATIONSHIP

Yesterday we looked at the example of Moses to understand the relationship between spiritual growth and Great Commission worship. Today we'll examine Moses' life as a picture of an intimate, committed relationship with God.

List two things that enhance your relationship with God and two things that interfere with your relationship with God.

	Enhance	Interfere
1.		1.
2.		2.

Before God allowed the people to enter the promised land, He wanted to test their faith, fortitude, and loyalty, so He kept them in the wilderness for several years. During this time Moses had several extraordinary encounters with God.

Read Exodus 19:16-22; 33:7-11. Explain the importance of Moses' spending time in the presence of God.

Why is it important for believers to spend time with God?

As He did with Moses, God wants to have an intimate, personal relationship with each of us. However, many people want the benefits of being intimate with God without actually being intimate with God. We're afraid of God. We're afraid of what that relationship might demand of us, how much time and effort it would take to establish, or how much control we might have to relinquish.

Scripture tells us when God manifested Himself on Mount Sinai, the Israelites were afraid of an encounter with the Almighty. Exodus 20:19 records their words: " 'You speak to us, and we will listen,' they said to Moses, 'but don't let God speak to us, or we will die.' "

We're the same way today. We understand God's directions for our lives and His desire for a personal relationship with us, but we're afraid of losing our lives—or at least the things in our lives that we place before God.

Moses, on the other hand, pursued God on the mountaintop and in the tent of meeting, and his life was transformed. Scripture tells us that Moses went up to Mount Sinai, where he enjoyed personal fellowship with God (see 19:20). And in the tent of meeting, "the LORD spoke with Moses face to face, just as a man speaks with his friend" (33:11).

List practical ways we can build an intimate relationship with God.

Like Moses, we have to spend time with God to develop an intimate, obedient relationship with Him. The Bible is full of verses that direct us in how to pray and tell us the importance of prayer. Paul's epistles give many instructions on prayer:

> Rejoice in hope; be patient in affliction;
> be persistent in prayer.
>
> Romans 12:12

> Pray at all times in the Spirit with every prayer and
> request, and stay alert in this with all perseverance
> and intercession for all the saints.
>
> Ephesians 6:18

> Don't worry about anything, but in everything,
> through prayer and petition with thanksgiving,
> let your requests be made known to God.
>
> Philippians 4:6

How would you describe your prayer life—routine and rushed or deep and intimate?

What adjustments would you have to make in your life to spend more time developing an intimate relationship with God?

A casual prayer life won't create the kind of intimate relationship that Moses had with God. A transformational relationship requires laying down your fears and spending time face-to-face with the God of the universe.

A RELATIONSHIP OF OBEDIENCE

So far we've learned two important facts from Moses' story.

1. Moses answered God's call on his life at the burning bush. In spite of his fears, he obeyed God, confronted Pharaoh, and led the Hebrews out of Egypt.

2. Moses spent face-to-face time building an intimate, transformational relationship with God.

As a result of Moses' obedient relationship with the Lord, the Israelites' lives were transformed. This didn't occur overnight. Even though they'd witnessed the Lord's miraculous saving works, they didn't experience the same kind of spiritual growth that Moses did. They were impatient, immature, and rebellious, continually complaining to Moses about their situation. They even rejected God and worshiped a golden calf (see Ex. 32). Later, because of their disbelief, God made them wander in the wilderness for 40 years before entering the promised land.

None of these obstacles prevented Moses from serving as God's ambassador to His people. Moses faithfully communicated God's Word and will to the Israelites and demanded their obedience to God's law. Later he issued this warning:

> After Moses finished reciting all these words to all
> Israel, he said to them, "Take to heart all these words
> I am giving as a warning to you today, so that you may
> command your children to carefully follow all the words
> of this law. For they are not meaningless words to you
> but they are your life, and by them you will live long in
> the land you are crossing the Jordan to possess."
> Deuteronomy 32:45-47

Look back at Moses' life and think about the ways God used this man. He went from doubting his ability to confronting Pharaoh. He led the Hebrew people out of bondage to the border of the promised land. He submitted his fears to God and allowed Him to develop an obedient, growing relationship that produced one of the greatest leaders in the pages of Scripture. Because of his obedience God used Moses to transform a population of slaves into a great nation.

Have you experienced a calling from God in your life? What is it?

How has your relationship with God transformed you?

How has your relationship with God influenced your ability
to worship and witness?

God has called you, as He called Moses, to be a worshiper and a witness as you
are transformed by an intimate relationship with Him. Have you boldly set aside
your fears and asked God to take over? Have you surrendered to His perfect will
and calling for your life? Have you entered an intimate relationship with the
One who created you? God wants you to know Him through a transformational
relationship with Him and then to move out in obedience as a Great Commission
worshiper and witness.

TODAY'S EVANGELISM EXPRESSION

Think about the ways God has transformed you through a personal relationship
with Him. Think about how that relationship has shaped your calling to witness
and worship.
• How is your relationship with God preparing you to encourage or lead others
  to know God and worship Him?
• What are ways you can communicate your story of transformation to others?
• Why is it important to be able to share your experience with others?

TODAY'S WORSHIP EXPRESSION

God wants all of His people to have an intimate, face-to-face relationship with
Him, the Creator of the universe. Spend time asking God to bring you closer
to Himself. Ask God to make His calling visible in your life so that you'll have
opportunities to lead others to become Great Commission worshipers as well.

DAY 5

WHAT JESUS HAS DONE FOR YOU

This week we've learned that Great Commission worship is transformational. God uses our obedience, repentance, spiritual growth, and relationship with Him to transform us. It's important to realize that true transformation can't be experienced by our own strength. It's only through the cross of Christ that spiritual transformation can take place at all.

The gospel says our morality, our success, or our good intentions don't bring us to God. In fact, the Bible says we're so corrupted with our own arrogant self-worship that even deeds that appear to be good are tainted. The gospel says we're incapable of doing enough good to be loved by God. There's only one way we could come to Him:

> While we were still helpless, at the appointed moment, Christ died for the ungodly. For rarely will someone die for a just person—though for a good person perhaps someone might even dare to die. But God proves His own love for us in that while we were still sinners, Christ died for us!
>
> Romans 5:6-8

What emotions do you experience when you read these verses? Why?

How does the gospel empower and embolden us?

Jesus lived the life you're incapable of living. He took all your sin on Himself when He died a cursed death on a cross. Whether you're good or bad is irrelevant. It's not your goodness that causes God to love and accept you. It's Jesus' good life and death in your place.

Therefore, we must place Jesus Christ at the focal point of all our worship and evangelism. He's the focal point of redemption. He's the focal point of resurrection. He's the focal point of eternal life. He's the focal point of fellowship with God. He's the focal point of our worship. And He's the focal point of our good news to the world. How we embrace the truth that Jesus is "the Lamb of God, who takes away the sin of the world" (John 1:29) will be revealed in our worship and evangelism.

What has Jesus done for you?

How should believers respond to all Jesus has done for them?

FILLED WITH THE SPIRIT

Peter was a fisherman, a leader, and Jesus' right-hand man. More importantly, Peter was a transformed Great Commission worshiper.

Peter interacted with Jesus at numerous times and in numerous ways. But when was he actually transformed by Jesus? You might think Peter's experience of walking on the water would have been his defining moment with Jesus. After Jesus got into the boat and calmed the sea, His disciples worshiped Him (see Matt. 14:33). What about the time Peter saw Moses, Elijah, and Abraham with Jesus on the mount of transfiguration (see Luke 9:28-36)? Surely that would have been the moment Peter experienced transformational worship. Or maybe trans-formational worship took place when Peter repented of denying Christ before the crucifixion (see John 21).

No. Peter's transformation didn't come until after Jesus' death and resurrection. It came because of what had happened to Jesus and what Peter experienced when 120 followers of Jesus gathered in an upper room. While Peter and the others were in a focused time of prayer and worship, God blessed them with His presence.

Read Acts 2:1-4. What does it mean to be filled with the Holy Spirit?

Why was Peter's experience with Jesus following the resurrection and the day of Pentecost the turning point for Peter?

Peter experienced transformational worship and was forever changed. Acts 2 goes on to tell us that Peter stood and began to preach to the crowd, proclaiming the death and resurrection of Jesus. As a result, the people cried out in repentance, and three thousand people were saved (see Acts 2:41).

INDIVIDUAL AND CORPORATE

There are two qualities about transformational worship that became evident on the day of Pentecost.

1. Transformational worship is for individuals. Transformation is deeply personal. It's something that must be experienced by each person as he or she worships the Lord. We can't experience the transforming power of the Holy Spirit for anyone else. It's a transformation that only God can do in your life.

Describe an experience with God that was transformational for you. How did it change you and your perception of God?

2. Transformation can also take place in a corporate context. As we experience God's transformational power as the body of Christ, we're able to worship more richly together. This is exactly what happened in Acts 2. The Holy Spirit came on each person individually, but the Spirit's presence and power impacted the entire group corporately. That's transformational worship. It's the power of God working in lives both individually and corporately.

What are some of the best times of worship you've experienced?

Are you experiencing worship both individually and corporately? What steps do you need to take to practice both?

EVIDENCE OF TRANSFORMATION

Peter wasn't the Teacher's pet of the disciples. For example, he had little faith when Jesus walked on water (see Matt. 14:22-33). In addition, he denied Jesus three separate times (see Matt. 26:69-75). But everything changed after Pentecost.

Read Acts 4:8-20. What evidence do you see of Peter's transformation after he was filled with the Spirit at Pentecost?

Peter had gotten himself in hot water for claiming that Jesus is the only name by which we can be saved. Why? Because the Roman government, like many groups in our culture today, believed in religious pluralism. They even had a building dedicated to it, called the Pantheon, to show their support for a diversity of religious philosophies.

Rome's problem with Christianity wasn't that it didn't want people to worship Jesus; it just couldn't have people saying Jesus was the only one who should be worshiped. But when Peter was told to stop preaching Jesus as the only way to God, he gave this response: "Whether it's right in the sight of God for us to listen to you rather than to God, you decide; for we are unable to stop speaking about what we have seen and heard" (Acts 4:19-20).

What had Peter seen and heard?

How do you explain Peter's boldness in the face of imprisonment or death?

Peter was essentially telling these Roman officials, "Look, we're not here to offend you, but we just saw Jesus die and then come back to life. So when asked to choose between listening to you or to Him, we're standing by the Guy who used to be dead and is now alive."

There's no way we could ever simply stumble on God. He had to show Himself to us. He had to come to us as one of us, tell us about Himself, then die and be resurrected to show that He's God.

Peter simply made an objective claim, the claim of a firsthand witness to events he'd seen. Those events transformed everything for Peter and changed the way he lived his life in public. Before when he'd been accused of being one of Jesus' followers, he'd said, "No, not me!" Now when the authorities told him to shut his mouth under the threat of imprisonment and death, he defied them and kept on preaching. Peter's boldness is clear, irrefutable evidence of a life that had been transformed by the power of God.

How does encountering Jesus in a transformational way enable and embolden us to carry out the Great Commission?

How does the gospel also push us toward worship?

At the exact same time the gospel brings us to our knees and humbles us to the core, it also produces boldness. The kind of boldness you see from people who have nothing to lose. People like Isaiah, David, Moses, and Peter.

TODAY'S EVANGELISM ASSIGNMENT

Last week you prepared a written testimony of your faith in Jesus Christ. This week prepare your transformation testimony. Review Today's Evangelism Expression in the previous days this week and record your account of the ways the Holy Spirit has transformed you since you became a believer.
• How have you grown spiritually?
• How have you learned to obey God's Word?
• How has your relationship with God deepened?
• How have you grown in the likeness of Jesus?

Record your story in a format you can share with someone. Practice presenting it to a friend or family member. Pray that God will bring someone into your life who needs to hear your story of spiritual transformation. Ask Him to give you boldness to share your transformational experience.

TODAY'S WORSHIP ASSIGNMENT

Reread Romans 5:6-8. Remind yourself throughout the day that it's not your goodness that causes God to love and accept you. It's Jesus' good life and sacrificial death in your place. Praise God today that there's nothing you can do to make Him love you any more or any less. His love is eternal and unconditional.

1. Bob Deffinbaugh, "Real Repentance" [online, cited 12 September 2012]. Available from the Internet: http://bible.org.
2. Robertson McQuilkin, *Living the Life 2* (Nashville: LifeWay Press, 2012), 42.
3. Ibid.

WEEK 2 GROUP EXPERIENCE

BREAK THE ICE

Use the following activity to introduce the topics covered in this week's study.

SUPPLIES NEEDED. A clear drinking glass, two or three ice cubes, and another glass filled with water

ACTIVITY. Place the ice cubes in the clear glass and display them so that all group participants can see them. Keep an eye on the ice cubes as you discuss the following questions.

What's required to facilitate the transformation of ice cubes into water?

What's required to facilitate our spiritual transformation as we move toward the likeness of Christ?

Pour the water into the glass holding the ice cubes. What happened to the ice cubes? Why?

What kinds of experiences or interactions typically speed and deepen our spiritual transformation?

Prepare for further group discussion by reading aloud the following passage.

> I will give you a new heart and put a new spirit within you;
> I will remove your heart of stone and give you a heart of
> flesh. I will place My Spirit within you and cause you to
> follow My statutes and carefully observe My ordinances.
> Ezekiel 36:26-27

DIG DEEPER

Use the following excerpts from the study material to move below the surface and engage in transformational conversations.

DAY 1. If you're a child of God, you experienced the work of the Holy Spirit at salvation. This was so much more than renovation. It was more than simply taking something dirty and cleaning it up to make it pretty. Your regeneration was a total change of your very nature from the inside out. Paul described it this way: "If anyone is in Christ, he is a new creation; old things have passed away, and look, new things have come" (2 Cor. 5:17).

What did Paul mean by "old things" and "new things"?

How did the Holy Spirit change you at the moment of your salvation?

Obedience is at the core of authentic, transformational worship and evangelism. We demonstrate our love—our worship—of God best when we do what He tells us to do. When we obey His Word, our worship becomes transformational.

What are some specific ways you've seen your obedience to God transform your life?

What happens when our obedience is directed toward ritual instead of toward genuine worship?

DAY 2. When we worship, we become aware of the presence and immensity of our sin. We get a glimpse of the way God views our sin, causing us to seek repentance.

How does sin affect your ability to experience genuine worship?

Describe a time when you experienced true repentance. Was it difficult? Explain.

Scripture gives several examples of repentance. One that stands out is found in 2 Samuel 11–12, the account of David's adultery with Bathsheba. This passage provides a humbling look at the way our sins affect our relationships with those around us and with God. But through David's sin and its consequences, we also get a glimpse of God's grace, love, and forgiveness. All of these factors eventually pointed David toward true repentance.

Why does a single sin often lead to other sins?

How have you seen this happen in your life?

DAY 3. God is glorified when He sees His work grow and develop in our lives. It's God who gives comfort, peace, contentment, and direction for life. As we worship and tell others about Him, we experience His comfort, His peace, and His love in powerful ways. And He gives us opportunities to walk with Him, talk with Him, trust Him, and declare His wonders to unbelievers around us.

In other words, God transforms our daily walk.

Describe what an ideal daily walk with God looks like.

Which of these elements are already present in your walk? Which need to be added?

DAY 4. A casual prayer life won't create the kind of intimate relationship that Moses had with God. A transformational relationship requires laying down your fears and spending time face-to-face with the God of the universe.

How would you describe your prayer life—routine and rushed or deep and intimate?

What adjustments would you have to make in your life to spend more time developing an intimate relationship with God?

Look back at Moses' life and think about the ways God used this man. He went from doubting his ability to confronting Pharaoh. He led the Hebrew people out of bondage to the border of the promised land. He submitted his fears to God and allowed Him to develop an obedient, growing relationship that produced one of the greatest leaders in the pages of Scripture. Because of his obedience God used Moses to transform a population of slaves into a great nation.

How has your relationship with God transformed you?

How has your relationship with God influenced your ability to be a Great Commission worshiper? A Great Commission witness?

DAY 5. There are two qualities about transformational worship that became evident on the day of Pentecost.

1. Transformational worship is for individuals. Transformation is deeply personal. It's something that must be experienced by each person as he or she worships the Lord. We can't experience the transforming power of the Holy Spirit for anyone else. It's a transformation that only God can do in your life.

How has your perception of God changed in recent years?

Describe a transformational experience you've had with God in recent years.

2. Transformation can also take place in a corporate context. As we experience God's transformational power as the body of Christ, we're able to worship more richly together.

What are some of the best times of worship you've experienced?

Are you experiencing worship both individually and corporately? What steps do you need to take to practice both?

APPLY TO LIFE

Discuss your experiences with the Evangelism Expression and Worship Expression at the end of each day's study material.

What emotions did you experience while preparing your transformational testimony this week?

If you're willing and as time allows, share your testimony of growing closer to the likeness of Christ in recent years.

The Worship Expression in day 5 included these instructions: "Praise God today that there's nothing you can do to make Him love you any more or any less. His love is eternal and unconditional." What emotions do you experience when you read those words? Why?

PRAY

As you conclude this group experience, spend time thanking God for the many ways He's changed your life and changed you as an individual. Don't be afraid to be specific.

GREAT COMMISSION WORSHIP IS RELATIONAL

Ernest Hemingway's short story "The Capital of the World" tells of a father and son's strained relationship.

The son, Paco, had sinned against his father and fled his home because of his shame. His father, however, loved the boy and set out on a journey to search for him. After looking all over Spain, Paco's father put an ad in a Madrid newspaper that read, "Paco: Meet at Hotel Montana noon Tuesday. All is forgiven. Papa."

On Tuesday at noon, the father arrived at Hotel Montana and was shocked by the sight before him. Eight hundred boys named Paco had shown up to find forgiveness, hoping the ad was for them.

This captivating story of a father's love for his son reminds us of Jesus' parable of the prodigal son (see Luke 15:11-32). And just like the eight hundred sons who showed up at the hotel, countless prodigal sons and daughters today have run from God yet are still desperate for a renewed relationship with the Father.

Fortunately, our Father in heaven hasn't given up on the search. He longs for our return. And when we come back to Him, He will forgive and restore us.

God made us to enjoy vibrant relationships. He's the God of relationships. When we have a relationship with the living God, we naturally engage in the Great Commandment and the Great Commission in order to worship Him and lead others to Him. As our vertical relationship with God grows stronger, it influences our horizontal relationships with everyone around us.

DAY 1

A VERTICAL RELATIONSHIP

Tom Hanks starred in the award-winning movie *Cast Away*. In the film Hanks portrayed Chuck, a man who was trapped on a remote, uninhabited island for 1,500 days after his FedEx® plane crashed during a flight across the Pacific Ocean.

Soon after the crash a package washed onto the shore of the island and caught Chuck's attention. In the package he found, among other things, a volleyball. One day Chuck accidentally stamped the ball with a bloody handprint that vaguely looked like a human face. After drawing in two eyes and a mouth, Chuck named the ball Wilson and began carrying it around the island with him. Eventually he began talking with Wilson as if the ball were a human companion.

The movie illustrates something very basic about humans: we were created for relationships. Our brains are hardwired for them. And even if all human contact is stripped away, we'll find companionship in something.

List several meaningful relationships in your life.

How is your relationship with God like your closest human relationships? How is it different?

Your most basic relationship in life is your relationship with God. This vertical relationship is your most important relationship, and it affects all of the horizontal relationships in your life. Yet it's possible to neglect or even abandon your relationship with God. This can be caused by any number of reasons: becoming spiritually numb because of sin, failing to spend time with God, or simply not trusting in His many promises. But when our relationship with God suffers, there's really only one major issue at play: our worship no longer points upward. We've neglected our vertical relationship with the One who matters most.

RELATIONAL WORSHIP

Relational worship is based on friendship, affinity, and a bond with God. The quest for a vertical relationship is actually the pursuit of vertical worship. And God is the One who initiates this relationship.

God nurtures our relationship as we worship Him. He's vitally interested in seeing us pursue a closer relationship through daily companionship with Him as the living Lord of the universe and as our loving Father. He wants this relationship with Him to be active, vibrant, intimate, and worshipful—a holy friendship. God doesn't walk or run ahead of us. He wants to walk with us through life. As we seek to know Him, He nurtures this relationship personally, individually, and lovingly. Look at the way Isaiah described this personal relationship:

> Jacob, why do you say,
> and Israel, why do you assert:
> "My way is hidden from the LORD,
> and my claim is ignored by my God"?
> Do you not know?
> Have you not heard?
> Yahweh is the everlasting God,
> the Creator of the whole earth.
> He never grows faint or weary;
> there is no limit to His understanding.
> He gives strength to the weary
> and strengthens the powerless.
> Youths may faint and grow weary,
> and young men stumble and fall,
> but those who trust in the LORD
> will renew their strength;
> they will soar on wings like eagles;
> they will run and not grow weary;
> they will walk and not faint.
>
> Isaiah 40:27-31

What truths in this passage have you experienced in your relationship with God?

Read the following passages and record key words that would encourage your pursuit of a vertical relationship with the Lord.

Psalm 18:2

Psalm 139:1-5

Isaiah 41:10

Ephesians 1:17-19

In the garden of Eden, God fashioned man from dust with the capacity to worship Him. He created Eve from Adam's rib with the same ability. God gave Adam and Eve a unique glimpse of perfect worship, and they received great pleasure from that worship. Because they hadn't yet sinned, they had minds and wills capable of making right choices, and they found total fulfillment in being with God.

In those moments worship was perfect. Imagine what perfect worship in the garden looked and felt like: closing their eyes each night in the arms of God and waking each morning after peaceful rest to find Him waiting for them. In that place, free from distractions and selfish pursuits, it was natural to love God. The couple was able to walk with God in perfect fellowship, knowing in their hearts that God was near and true.

Then came the tragic events of Genesis 3, when Adam and Eve chose to sin. In doing so, they placed a wedge between them and God, disrupting the perfect fellowship they'd enjoyed with Him. Only God's merciful intervention would make it possible for people to relate to Him again.

Even though believers today are fallen creatures, how does God allow us to enjoy His presence?

How have you experienced growth in your relationship with God as you've walked with Him?

Even after the fall, God is still in the business of building relationships. He wants to have a relationship with us that's holy and perfect. Although we can't experience perfect worship until we arrive in heaven, we can enjoy His presence, thrill at His wonder, experience His love, and love Him supremely. In return, God nurtures us, gives us peace, and cares for us, just as He did with Adam and Eve.

Here's an important principle of vertical worship: our worship of God is the foundation of our relationship with God. And the quality of our relationship with God is in direct proportion to our worship of Him.

BECOMING A WORSHIPER OF GOD

Maybe you're confused about all of this. How can you have a relationship with a God you can't physically see or touch? How can the perfect God love you and accept your worship even though you've sinned? The fact is, you can establish a deeply personal relationship with God right now, right where you are. Here's a simple look at how to become a worshiper of God.

1. **REALIZE YOU'RE A SINNER.** God's Word teaches us that we're all sinners. And it's because of our sin that all people from every generation experience death (see Rom. 6:23). Even though we're sinners, God loves us so much that He sent His Son to live on this earth, die on a cross, and rise victorious over death so that we could become worshipers (see Rom. 5:8-9). Jesus lived the perfect life we couldn't live and died in our place to pay for our sin.

2. **ASK JESUS TO FORGIVE YOU OF YOUR SINS.** The next step in becoming a worshiper of God involves repentance. This is recognizing the wrong you've done and being sorry about it. It involves feeling regret about sin or past actions and changing your ways or habits. It involves living for God instead of self. This is transformational worship in action.

3. **ACCEPT JESUS AS YOUR SAVIOR AND LORD.** God sent Jesus into this world for the sole purpose of providing a way for you to have a loving relationship with God. The Bible teaches if we confess with our lips that Jesus is Lord and believe in our hearts that God raised Him from the dead, we can become genuine worshipers of God. God removes all the sin from our lives, and we stand before Him as justified by faith. The relationship with God begins that we were made to enjoy (see Rom. 10:9-10).

Describe a time in your life when you took the three previous steps.

If you haven't taken these steps, you can take them now. If you feel that you need guidance, talk to a pastor or a Christian friend.

If you already have a vertical relationship with God, what are two ways you could strengthen it?

God secures your relationship with Him in heaven through the shed blood of Jesus Christ. The relationship God wants to share with you is a companionship that begins here on earth and endures forever. It's an eternal relationship.

TODAY'S EVANGELISM EXPRESSION

Take time to evaluate your vertical relationship with your Creator.
- Is it noticeable? Does it produce fruit? If it's difficult for you to recognize your upward relationship with God, others aren't noticing anything either.
- Where do you struggle most in your vertical relationship with God? Trust? Obedience? Giving in to temptation? Spending time with God?
- How can you tell others about your vertical relationship with God without coming across as self-righteous or arrogant?
- Think about people in your life who are witnesses of your relationship with God. What are they seeing?

TODAY'S WORSHIP EXPRESSION

Spend some time evaluating your vertical worship of God. Is it influencing your vertical relationship with Him? Pray that God will begin to draw you toward a deeper relationship with Him as you continue this week of study.

DAY 2

DESIRE, DEPEND ON, AND DELIGHT IN GOD

Our vertical relationship with God focuses entirely on one person—God Himself. Yet God focuses on meeting us at the point of our greatest need. This principle is most clearly seen in our worship of God.

The more God reveals Himself to us, the more we love Him. The more we love Him, the more we learn about Him. The more we know and learn about Him, the more we worship Him. The more we worship Him, the stronger our relationship with Him grows.

How have you experienced this progression in your life?

Are you encouraged to realize that God initiates the growth of your relationship when He reveals Himself to you? Why or why not?

This worship-driven relationship includes three essential elements: a desire for God, a dependence on God, and a delight in God. Let's look at all three today.

DESIRE FOR GOD

The purpose for the creation of the world and the revelation of Jesus both center on God's plan for intimate relationship with those He created. To bring about these relationships, God strategically places in the heart of each person an impulse or a desire to seek, know, comprehend, value, pursue, and love Him. A. W. Tozer has said, "We pursue God because, and only because, He has first put an urge within us that spurs us to the pursuit."[1] Because God has placed this impulse in our hearts, we can know Him and enjoy a relationship with Him that's personal and intentional.

A desire for God is the fuel that builds our relationship with Him. God made us for relationship, friendship, communion, camaraderie, and companionship. Our relationship with God matures as we spend time with Him in worship and prayer. The desire to experience God emerges as a reaction to our own personal instincts. We naturally respond to being loved by showing love. God loves us, so we naturally want to show love to Him in response.

Read Psalm 42:1-4. When in your life have you experienced a thirst for God? Describe the experience.

A desire for God is a defining reality of worship. God wants to be known on an intimate basis. He wants to enjoy an open, honest relationship with us.

DEPENDENCE ON GOD

Dependence is another defining reality of authentic worship. We depend on God for everything. He's our counselor, companion, caregiver, and guardian. God is committed to building a loving, meaningful, grace-filled relationship with His children as we rely on Him for our needs.

We depend on God for three things: to be our provider, protector, and giver of peace.

PROVIDER. God is Jehovah-Jireh, our provider. He places food on our tables and cares for our physical, emotional, and spiritual needs. His Word says the righteous will not go hungry or go begging for bread (see Ps. 37:25; Prov. 10:3). He gives us a home, a place to sleep, and shelter from the elements of life. We serve a God who meets our every need.

List practical ways God has met your physical, emotional, or spiritual needs in the past week.

Do you trust God to provide for you? Why or why not?

PROTECTOR. God is also our protector. The psalmist understood this principle as he sought God during a time of imminent danger:

> Who is God besides Yahweh?
> And who is a rock? Only our God.
> God—He clothes me with strength
> and makes my way perfect.
> He makes my feet like the feet of a deer
> and sets me securely on the heights.
> He trains my hands for war;
> my arms can bend a bow of bronze.
> You have given me the shield of Your salvation;
> Your right hand upholds me,
> and Your humility exalts me.
> You widen a place beneath me for my steps,
> and my ankles do not give way.
> You have clothed me with strength for battle;
> You subdue my adversaries beneath me.
> The LORD lives—may my rock be praised!
> The God of my salvation is exalted.
> Therefore I will praise You, Yahweh,
> among the nations;
> I will sing about Your name.
>
> Psalm 18:31-36,39,46,49

How do you see God as your protector in your everyday life?

God protects us spiritually, emotionally, and physically. He protects us from those who would speak evil and seek to damage our reputation, integrity, and character. God is our protector.

GIVER OF PEACE. God grants us His peace to settle our anxious spirits. The apostle Paul reminds us to "let the peace of the Messiah, to which you were also called in one body, control your hearts" (Col. 3:15). When we live in God's peace, there's no apprehension, distress, worry, dread, panic, fright, or trepidation. He guards and protects our hearts and keeps us close to His side.

Read Philippians 4:6-7. Describe a time in your life when you personally experienced God's peace.

God provides for our needs, protects us, and gives us the peace and confidence that we're free from guilt, conflict, disagreement, war, anger, envy, covetousness, resentfulness, and jealousy. God meets every hunger of our soul and grants total, unreserved peace, calm, and quietness of heart.

Which component of your dependence on God has recently been the most apparent in your life: God as provider, protector, or giver of peace? Explain.

DELIGHT IN GOD

The third element in building a relationship with our loving God involves delight. There's a difference between desire and delight. Desire implies a hunger for God—a pursuit to know Him. Delight describes our reaction to this relationship with Him. It implies great joy, pleasure, happiness, and enjoyment. John Piper has said, "God is most glorified in us when we are most satisfied in Him."[2]

What does it mean that God is glorified in us?

How have you experienced joy that only God can provide?

A relationship with God is something He intended us to experience and enjoy. The psalmist wrote:

> In Your presence is abundant joy;
> in Your right hand are eternal pleasures.
>
> Psalm 16:11

> I will come to the altar of God,
> to God, my greatest joy.
>
> Psalm 43:4

God's message in 1 John was written "so that our joy may be complete" (1 John 1:4). Similarly, the apostle Paul encouraged the brethren under the siege of persecution to "rejoice in the Lord always" (Phil. 4:4).

The secret to a vital, intimate relationship with God is to find our joy in Him. When we do, God responds by giving us more joy. Our response will become an outgrowth of what God is doing in our hearts. And as C. S. Lewis wrote, "All enjoyment spontaneously overflows into praise."[3]

We delight in God because He created us to enjoy Him. When we delight in our relationship with Him, that relationship results in the worship of the One who created us for His glory.

TODAY'S EVANGELISM EXPRESSION

Do you think the people in your life whom you meet on a daily or weekly basis are seeing in your life a desire for, dependence on, and delight in God? Record any evidence they would see for—
• your desire for God;
• your dependence on God;
• your delight in God.

TODAY'S WORSHIP EXPRESSION

Wherever you are, find a quiet place and spend at least five minutes delighting in God. Write a note to God expressing your love and commitment.

DAY 3

RELATING TO GOD THROUGH PRAYER

You've probably heard the phrase "Absence makes the heart grow fonder." But does it? Possibly in some scenarios, but most of the time absence just makes the heart lonelier. The reality is that relationships grow through personal interaction. Even when two persons are physically away from each other, they're still likely to interact through e-mails, texts, or phone conversations.

The same is true in our relationship with God. We can't expect our relationship to thrive if there's no communication. Abiding in Christ through prayer is the greatest expression of a Christian's relationship with God. It's essential if we truly expect to become Great Commission worshipers.

Describe your prayer life in a typical week.

How do you think a stronger prayer life could improve your relationship with God?

Growing your vertical relationship with God requires an abiding commitment to prayer. Today we'll look at two Scripture passages from two different perspectives in order to understand the nature and power of prayer.

THE PURPOSE AND PRACTICE OF PRAYER

In the Sermon on the Mount, Jesus gave His listeners some instructions on prayer and then taught them to follow a particular pattern for prayer. Today we know that example as the model prayer.

Read Matthew 6:5-13. How is praying, as described in verses 5-8, meaningless or disruptive in enriching a relationship with God?

Which warning in verses 5-8 presents the greatest challenge for you?

In verses 9-13 Jesus presented a model for praying. He began His prayer by addressing His Father in heaven (see v. 9). Your view of God shapes the way you pray. He is our holy Father who resides in heaven. But unlike some earthly fathers, God displays His perfect love, provision, and protection over our lives.

In verse 10 Jesus prayed for God's will to be done. This verse has implications for evangelism. Because His kingdom has already come in the hearts of believers, we're instructed to pray that it will continue to go forth and take hold of hearts that do not yet know the Father.

Jesus' prayer also encourages us to rely on God for provision (see v. 11). As an earthly father is called to provide for his family, Scripture shows us that God provides for our every need (see Pss. 68:6; 104:14; 1 Tim. 6:17).

In prayer we also ask for forgiveness. Many translations of Matthew 6:12 use the words *debt* and *debtors* to describe sin and those who've sinned against us. Our sins and others' sins toward us are viewed as obligations. We must forgive those who've sinned against us if we're to receive forgiveness from God for our sins (see vv. 14-15).

Finally, verse 13 shows us the importance of praying for protection from the rise of temptation in our hearts. We should place our confidence in God to lead us to paths of righteousness, knowing that He holds all power.

What elements of this model of prayer do you have trouble practicing? Why?

Using this prayer as a model, how would you summarize the purpose and practice of prayer to a new believer?

The most striking feature of Jesus' prayer is that it reveals prayer as a relationship with the Father. Prayer isn't simply a tug-of-war match between you and God in which you try to use prayer to meet your selfish needs. Prayer also isn't a magic wand to brandish whenever you get in trouble. Prayer exists to honor God, to bring Him glory, and to display our trust in His sovereignty over our lives. James issued this warning:

> You do not have because you do not ask. You ask and
> don't receive because you ask with wrong motives,
> so that you may spend it on your evil desires.
>
> James 4:2-3

God desires a personal relationship with us. The purpose of prayer is to cultivate that relationship as we talk to God, listen to Him, bring our minds and wills into conformity with His, and ask for His will and purposes to be accomplished on earth as they are in heaven. Gregory Frizzell explains:

> Prayer is not primarily what we can get out of God, but
> what He purposes to do in and through us for His own
> pleasure. Prayer is a major way we come to know Him and
> hear His voice. Through prayer, we abide in Him and allow
> Him to live through us. Prayer is how Christ purifies His
> bride and builds His kingdom. The great secret of prayer
> is to align ourselves to God's purposes rather than seeking
> to align Him to ours. … Until you are totally convinced of
> the importance of a lifestyle of prayer, you are not likely
> to take the necessary steps to achieve one. … Above
> everything else, God desires a close personal relationship
> with each of His children. Yet, it is impossible to develop
> this relationship without spending significant time with
> God. Prayer is the primary way you spend meaningful time
> with the Savior. Through prayer, God purposes to establish
> and deepen your personal relationship with Him.[4]

What evidence in your life reveals that you're growing in your relationship with God through prayer?

What changes do you need to make to spend more time with God?

Prayer serves as the primary means by which we communicate with God. When we understand this and spend time developing our relationship with God through prayer, our ways, desires, and motives will begin to align with His.

PRAYERS OF CONFESSION

In day 1 we saw that sin blocked Adam and Eve's fellowship with God. The same thing is true of Christians today. When we sin, we don't lose our relationship with God, but we harm that relationship by creating distance between God and us. That's why prayers of confession are so important for a growing disciple.

Read Psalm 51. What are your initial impressions about David's prayer of repentance?

Why is this type of prayer crucial to a relationship with God?

Many people don't realize the depth of their sin, but Scripture is clear about its severity. Because sin separates us from God, we stand under His righteous condemnation. David expressed it this way:

> I am conscious of my rebellion,
> and my sin is always before me.
> Against You—You alone—I have sinned
> and done this evil in Your sight.
> So You are right when You pass sentence;
> You are blameless when You judge.
>
> Psalm 51:3-4

Furthermore, we can do nothing to atone for our sins because even our righteous acts are trivial in the sight of God. Only He can cleanse us from sin:

Indeed, I was guilty when I was born;
I was sinful when my mother conceived me.
Surely You desire integrity in the inner self,
and You teach me wisdom deep within.
Purify me with hyssop, and I will be clean;
wash me, and I will be whiter than snow.

Psalm 51:5-7

On the other hand, some believe their sin is too big or too grievous for God to forgive. They can't imagine that a good and just God would forgive heinous crimes that are committed in complete rebellion.

David knew the seriousness of his sin. But he was also confident if he sincerely confessed his sins, however big they were, he would find God waiting with open arms, ready to forgive.

Which can you better relate to—not realizing the depth of your sin or thinking your sin is too big for God to handle? Why?

If we want to have a thriving relationship with God, we must come to Him openly and honestly. We must agree with Him that we've sinned and fallen short of His design for us and that this sin separates us from Him: "All have sinned and fall short of the glory of God" (Rom. 3:23). Psalm 51 shows that David had a healthy understanding of the depths of his moral failure, but he held on tightly to the hope of God's forgiveness and cleansing.

It's imperative, therefore, that believers hold on to the same hope David had. Jesus' death in our place covers even the worst of sins. If we confess our sins in prayer, God will forgive and draw us closer in a love relationship with Him. The apostle John assured us, "If we confess our sins, He is faithful and righteous to forgive us our sins and to cleanse us from all unrighteousness" (1 John 1:9).

Identify a time when you realized the seriousness of your sin. What caused you to see your sin from God's perspective?

How confident are you that God will forgive you when you confess your sins to Him? Explain.

No matter what you've done, God will forgive if you confess and repent. A growing, intimate relationship with your Heavenly Father requires that you pray like David:

> God, create a clean heart for me
> and renew a steadfast spirit within me.
>
> Psalm 51:10

TODAY'S EVANGELISM EXPRESSION

Reread verses 12-13 of David's prayer in Psalm 51 and think about how well your life reflects these Great Commission truths. How are you showing people God's perfect ways so that they can return to God as David did?

Over the past couple of weeks, you've identified people in your life who need to hear the gospel. Today spend a few minutes praying for these people by name. Ask God to give you a "willing spirit" (Ps. 51:12) to share with these individuals what He's done for you.

TODAY'S WORSHIP EXPRESSION

Continue your prayer time with God, thanking Him for the power of prayer and for the avenue it provides for open communication with Him. Ask God to make you fully aware of your sin and to lead you toward repentance, breaking down the sin barrier and restoring your fellowship with Him.

DAY 4

HORIZONTAL RELATIONSHIPS WITH BELIEVERS

In the past few days we've seen that Great Commission worship is vertically relational. God designed our relationship with Him to be personal and to reflect our worship of Him.

While Great Commission worship affects our vertical relationship with God, it also affects our horizontal relationships with others. In other words, Great Commission worship has incredibly important implications for the relationships we have on earth. God made us to enjoy these relationships and to bring glory to Him through our interactions with others.

What do you enjoy most about your relationships with others?

Why are horizontal relationships important?

How do vertical worship and horizontal relationships complement each other?

It seems fairly natural that our worship is directed upward to God, but Great Commission worship doesn't stop there. It involves application. We have to ask, *How does my upward worship impact other people in my life?* So when we discuss horizontal relationships, we're specifically talking about the application of worship to our daily lives. Our horizontal relationships reflect the depth, duration, and quality of our worship of God.

When you understand horizontal relationships from the perspective of Great Commission worship, you'll find that it's literally lifestyle worship in action. It's a 24-hour, seven-day-a-week commitment. If we've been formed and shaped by Great Commission worship and our hearts have truly been transformed by the power of the Holy Spirit, then everything we are and do in life should reflect our love for God and the people He created.

CONSIDER YOUR BROTHERS AND SISTERS

There are two categories of horizontal relationships, both of which are crucial in developing God-honoring worship and evangelism. Today we'll talk about relationships with other believers, and tomorrow we'll discuss the importance of relationships with those who haven't yet professed Christ as their Savior.

Read Romans 12:9-21. List five things you should do and five things you shouldn't do to build stronger relationships with believers.

Do	Don't Do
1.	1.
2.	2.
3.	3.
4.	4..
5.	5.

These passages show us how to cultivate God-honoring relationships in our daily living. Paul wrote, "Be devoted to one another in brotherly love. Honor one another above yourselves" (Rom. 12:10, NIV). For a believer, a lifestyle of worship is expressed in loving and respecting our brothers and sisters in Christ. It's revealed in our ability to treat everyone fairly and selflessly.

Being devoted to one another and honoring others above ourselves are values that run contrary to our culture's humanistic, secular values. We live in a culture that's self-centered in every area of life. Driven by the desire for success, many people sacrifice everything, including their closest relationships, to achieve it.

In contrast, the principle of devotion to one another in love is at the core of building relationships and unity among believers. If practiced on a regular basis, it will revolutionize our worship and evangelism endeavors. Our devotion, loyalty, fidelity, dedication, and commitment to one another build up the body of Christ in love and provide opportunities to serve and worship with one another. We're fulfilled when we see others become all God intended for them to be by reaching their goals, growing in grace, and developing their skills for ministry.

Name specific ways you're showing love and devotion to other believers.

In what areas of your life are you failing to minister to your brothers and sisters in Christ?

How do your relationships with fellow believers reflect positively or negatively on the cause of Christ?

Our horizontal relationships with believers begin and end with our love and devotion to them. Jesus taught us:

> I give you a new command: Love one another. Just as I have loved you, you must also love one another. By this all people will know that you are My disciples, if you have love for one another.
>
> John 13:34-35

We're also to reach out to them, serve them, and build relationships with our fellow believers. Paul issued this challenge:

> May the God who gives endurance and encouragement allow you to live in harmony with one another, according to the command of Christ Jesus, so that you may glorify the God and Father of our Lord Jesus Christ with a united mind and voice. Therefore accept one another, just as the Messiah also accepted you, to the glory of God.
>
> Romans 15:5-7

How does caring fellowship with other believers bring glory to God?

Fellowship with believers isn't just about having a good time. The body of Christ represents God on earth. When unbelievers see church members arguing and hating, they are repulsed because they see nothing different from the rest of the world. However, when they see us love and care for one another, they're attracted to our Heavenly Father, the source of all good things, and He's glorified. We can pray and work to make sure they too become His worshipers.

PRAY FOR YOUR BROTHERS AND SISTERS

Another foundational component in building healthy relationships among believers is prayer. Just as prayer is crucial to a growing relationship with God, it's also important for building relationships with our fellow believers.

There are two ways we can build relationships with believers by using the power of prayer. The first is praying *with* other believers.

Read Acts 1:12-14; 4:31-35. When did you last experience a time of intense, meaningful prayer with other believers?

How did that time strengthen your vertical relationship with God? Your horizontal relationships with other believers?

Last week we looked at the Holy Spirit's role in spiritual transformation, using the disciples' upper-room experience as an example. That passage is also a perfect example of how relationships, both vertical and horizontal, can be strengthened through prayer.

Acts 1:14 says, "All these were continually united in prayer," and verse 15 says about 120 were present. Their praying was unrelenting and unwavering. They prayed with one mind and one heart, and there was unity among them. God used believers, united in prayer and worship, to become partners in ministry together for the purpose of spreading the good news.

Prayer doesn't simply dry up when we're alone. Our prayers can continue to build relationships among believers even when we aren't together. The second way we can build relationships through prayer is by praying *for* other believers.

When we intercede for other Christians, we ask God to grant our requests for them according to His will. We first see the idea of being a mediator through prayer in the Old Testament with Abraham, Moses, David, Daniel, and many others. The New Testament also shows that Jesus interceded for His disciples.

Read John 17:15-26. What are some things Jesus prayed for His disciples?

What did Jesus pray for present-day believers?

As Jesus interceded for His disciples, we can pray for other believers. Paul wrote that the Holy Spirit intercedes for us so that we can pray more effectively (see Rom. 8:26). The writer of Hebrews admonishes us to "approach the throne of grace with boldness" (Heb. 4:16).

Read Colossians 1:3-12. What are some things Paul prayed for the Colossian believers?

How can praying for believers strengthen relationships?

Praying for believers shows the love and devotion we talked about earlier. In his letter to the church at Colossae, Paul encouraged the believers by telling them that he'd been in continual prayer for them. Paul was committed to intercede for others in prayer. As he prayed, he believed God would work in their lives to bring them to a greater knowledge of Him, produce fruit in their lives, and transform their character in the likeness of Christ.

Paul not only prayed for believers, but he also asked them to do the same for him.

Read the following verses and briefly identify what Paul asked his fellow believers to pray for.

Romans 15:31

Ephesians 6:19-20

Colossians 4:2-4

To what extent is praying for others a part of your normal prayer life?

Intercessory prayer is designed to be a key part of a believer's life. It's not just for the superspiritual or for church leaders. Scripture encourages all believers to intercede for others (see Eph. 6:18; Jas. 5:16). We're blessed to be able to come before our Maker with prayers of concern and thanksgiving on behalf of our brothers and sisters in Christ.

TODAY'S EVANGELISM EXPRESSION

Think about believers who relate to you and your family. Are you praying for those people? Make a list of several believers and commit to pray for them. If you have a large list, you can do this on a rotation. If your list is small, you can pray for all of these believers on a daily basis. As you intercede for them, ask God to bless them, to bring them to a greater knowledge of Him, and to use them for His purposes and according to His perfect will.

TODAY'S WORSHIP EXPRESSION

Choose one of your favorite hymns or praise choruses and reflect on the greatness of God. Thank Him that even though He's far above us and perfectly holy, He's made a way for us to come to Him boldly in prayer.

DAY 5

HORIZONTAL RELATIONSHIPS WITH UNBELIEVERS

There's a good chance that if you asked someone whether they're a member of a social-networking Web site, their answer would be yes. Over the past several years social networks have become dominant influences in modern society.

Billions of people around the world use social networking to reconnect with old relationships, make new relationships, share information or opinions, stay up-to-date on worldwide happenings, promote their businesses, find jobs, buy vehicles, or even find love. Social-networking sites bring together people with common interests and expose members to new ideas from around the world. The popularity of these Web sites forces corporations of all shapes and sizes to alter their business strategies to take advantage of this ever-changing cultural phenomenon.

These networks, often free and easy to join, have restructured the way we form relationships and communicate. But they also expose the importance of our innate need and desire to stay connected and form relationships with people.

Who is the one person in your life with whom you have the closest relationship?

What makes this relationship so close?

As we discussed yesterday, it's important to pursue healthy relationships with believers. But it's just as important to build healthy relationships with unbelievers. One crucial way we can apply Great Commission worship is to intentionally interact with people who don't know Christ as their Savior.

WITNESS ON DISPLAY

Love your neighbors. That's what Jesus tells us in the Great Commandment: "Love your neighbor as yourself" (Matt. 22:39). But do we really do that? The apostle Paul also reminds us, "Love does no wrong to a neighbor. Love, therefore, is the fulfillment of the law" (Rom. 13:10). We're sometimes really good at building relationships with our brothers and sisters in Christ, especially those we see every week, but it's much more difficult to interact with the neighbor across the street who doesn't claim to know Jesus.

The greatest and most consistent witness you'll have isn't a one-time encounter with the person you've never met before who sits beside you on a plane. It's the day-in-and-day-out relationship and testimony you display to your lost neighbor, coworker, family member, or friend.

Name three places in your life where you consistently interact with unbelievers.

1.

2.

3.

How do you think these people would describe you?

Do you find it easy or difficult to develop relationships with unbelievers? Explain.

The testimony we have around other people is of utmost importance. People are watching how we act and react in the normal ebb and flow of life. In fact, unsaved people of all cultures largely base what they understand about Christ on our testimony as worship-evangelists in our workplaces, in our schools, with our friends, and around our families.

What are some practical ways to reach out to people who don't know Jesus?

Why is reaching out to an unbeliever we see on a daily basis such an important component of both our worship and our witness?

Our daily actions toward all people, believers and nonbelievers, should reflect an understanding of and commitment to lifestyle worship-evangelism. Our lifestyle worship-evangelism isn't demonstrated by the number of programs at our church, the worship concerts we host for our friends, or the scores of block parties and evangelism efforts we have in a given period of time. As important as those things might be in the life and body of the church or in building the kingdom of God, worship and witness are best demonstrated in how we react to, reach out to, treat, manage, talk with, and pray for people.

PRAYING FOR YOUR NEIGHBOR

God wants us to pray for the unbelieving generation in the same way He wants us to intercede for our brother and sister in Christ. The first part of Romans 10 shows Paul's heart for and commitment to the unbelieving Jews:

> My heart's desire and prayer to God concerning them is for their salvation! I can testify about them that they have zeal for God, but not according to knowledge. Because they disregarded the righteousness from God and attempted to establish their own righteousness, they have not submitted themselves to God's righteousness. For Christ is the end of the law for righteousness to everyone who believes.
>
> Romans 10:1-4

The most amazing thing about these verses is the context that surrounds it. Paul was referring to the Jews in this passage—the same people who despised and rejected Jesus as the true Messiah. Paul's desire and prayer were for them to turn from their sin and embrace salvation in Christ. But this was no easy task. Their hearts were hardened because "they disregarded the righteousness from God and attempted to establish their own righteousness" (v. 3). Because of their strict adherence to the law, they didn't think they needed to be saved from anything. They placed their faith in family heritage, traditions, and works but not in the redeeming work of Jesus Christ. But in spite of this, Paul still prayed.

What are people today placing their faith in rather than Jesus?

Many people today find themselves in a similar situation to the Jews. Some don't believe in God at all. Many seek to earn heavenly rewards through good works. Others have rejected biblical faith, placing their confidence in what they perceive as scientific facts. Yet God loves all of those who are lost and wants them to come to Him: "The Lord ... is patient with you, not wanting any to perish but all to come to repentance" (2 Pet. 3:9). One way we can join His redemptive work is to pray faithfully for the lost people in our lives.

But instead of trusting God to work through our prayers, we sometimes question God: "Why would we pray for an unbelieving generation that's rejected You? And if You're the One who calls people to Yourself, why do You need us to pray?"

How would you answer those questions?

What's your present attitude toward prayer for the lost?

In what ways are you not trusting God in prayer?

What are some things believers should pray for in the lives of unbelievers?

Paul wrote in his first letter to his fellow minister Timothy, "I urge that petitions, prayers, intercessions, and thanksgivings be made for everyone. ... This is good, and it pleases God our Savior, who wants everyone to be saved and to come to the knowledge of the truth" (1 Tim. 2:1-4). As a converted Jew, Paul was greatly burdened by the hardened hearts of his fellow Jews. So he prayed. He didn't ask why; he just trusted in a God much bigger than himself. Paul desperately desired for them to recognize, as he had, Jesus as the promised Messiah.

Notice that Paul specifically instructs us to pray for unbelievers' salvation and "the knowledge of the truth" (v. 4), that is, the truth about Jesus. With that goal in mind, we can pray for God's blessing and healing in their lives so that they might see God's goodness and turn to Him. We can pray that their sin will leave them empty so that they long for the One who can satisfy their needs. We can pray that God will bring believers into their lives who can influence them for Christ. When we're faithful to pray for unbelievers, we often find that our prayers pave the way for us to share the gospel when God gives us opportunities.

TODAY'S EVANGELISM EXPRESSION

Yesterday you made a list of believers and committed to pray for those who relate to you and your family. Today make a list of unbelievers with whom you come in contact on a daily basis. Organize your list so that you pray for at least one believer and one unbeliever each day.

TODAY'S WORSHIP EXPRESSION

Praying for an unbeliever's salvation lays the groundwork for the Holy Spirit to work in someone's life. Ask God to use your prayers to build a God-honoring horizontal relationship with a future brother or sister in Christ.

Praise God for the work He's doing in your life through this study. Ask Him to show Himself to you in a mighty way as you worship and study His Word in this week's worship services.

1. A. W. Tozer, *The Pursuit of God* (Harrisburg, PA: Christian, 1946; repr., Camp Hill, PA: Wingspread, 2006), 11.
2. John Piper, *Desiring God,* rev. ed. (Colorado Springs: Multnomah, 2011), 309.
3. C. S. Lewis, *Reflections on the Psalms* (Orlando: Harcourt, 1986), 94.
4. Gregory R. Frizzell, *How to Develop a Powerful Prayer Life* (Memphis: The Master Design, 1999), 2–3.

WEEK 3 GROUP EXPERIENCE

BREAK THE ICE

Use the following activity to introduce the topics covered in this week's study.

SUPPLIES NEEDED. Several long strips of cloth (long socks will work)

ACTIVITY. Use the cloth strip to connect yourself with another member by tying your wrist or ankle to theirs. Once you're connected, stand up with your partner and walk around the room for two or three minutes. As you walk, ask other participants what they've enjoyed most about their week. After two or three minutes, return to your seat and untie the cloth strip. Then discuss the following questions.

In what ways were you impacted or hindered while physically connected to another person?

What does it mean to be relationally connected with other church members?

What does it mean to be relationally connected with God?

In what ways have you been affected by those connections in recent months?

Prepare for further group discussion by reading aloud the following passage.

> May the God who gives endurance and encouragement allow you to live in harmony with one another, according to the command of Christ Jesus, so that you may glorify the God and Father of our Lord Jesus Christ with a united mind and voice. Therefore accept one another, just as the Messiah also accepted you, to the glory of God.
>
> Romans 15:5-7

Use the following excerpts from the study material to move below the surface and engage in transformational conversations.

DAY 1. Your most basic relationship in life is your relationship with God. This vertical relationship is your most important relationship, and it affects all of the horizontal relationships in your life.

What words best describe your relationship with God? Why?

Which of your horizontal relationships currently have the biggest impact on your life?

God nurtures our relationship as we worship Him. He's vitally interested in seeing us pursue a closer relationship through daily companionship with Him as the living Lord of the universe and as our loving Father. He wants this relationship with Him to be active, vibrant, intimate, and worshipful—a holy friendship.

What emotions do you experience when you read those words?

DAY 2. Dependence is another defining reality of worship. We depend on God for everything. He's our counselor, companion, caregiver, and guardian. God is committed to building a loving, meaningful, grace-filled relationship with His children as we rely on Him for our needs.

We depend on God for three things: to be our provider, protector, and giver of peace.

Do you trust God to provide for you? Why or why not?

Read Philippians 4:6-7. Describe a time in your life when you personally experienced God's peace.

Which component of your dependence on God has recently been the most apparent in your life: God as provider, protector, or giver of peace? Explain.

DAY 3. God desires a personal relationship with us. The purpose of prayer is to cultivate that relationship as we talk to God, listen to Him, bring our minds and wills into conformity with His, and ask for His will and purposes to be accomplished on earth as they are in heaven.

Read Matthew 6:5-13. Which warning in verses 5-8 presents the greatest challenge for you?

Read Psalm 51. What are your initial impressions about David's prayer of repentance?

Why is this type of prayer crucial to a relationship with God?

DAY 4. While Great Commission worship affects our vertical relationship with God, it also affects our horizontal relationships with others. In other words, Great Commission worship has incredibly important implications for the relationships we have on earth. God made us to enjoy these relationships and to bring glory to Him through our interactions with others.

What do you enjoy most about your relationships with others?

How do vertical worship and horizontal relationships complement each other?

Intercessory prayer is designed to be a key part of a believer's life. It's not just for the superspiritual or for church leaders. Scripture encourages all believers to intercede for others (see Eph. 6:18; Jas. 5:16). We're blessed to be able to come before our Maker with prayers of concern and thanksgiving on behalf of our brothers and sisters in Christ.

To what extent is praying for others a part of your normal prayer life?

DAY 5. It's extremely important to pursue healthy relationships with believers. But it's just as important to build healthy relationships with unbelievers. One crucial way we can apply Great Commission worship is to intentionally interact with people who don't know Christ as their Savior.

Do you find it easy or difficult to develop relationships with unbelievers? Explain.

APPLY TO LIFE

Discuss your experiences with the Evangelism Expression and Worship Expression at the end of each day's study material.

Describe what you encountered while praying for believers and unbelievers throughout the week.

What have you learned about prayer in general through your experiences in this study?

How have you been motivated to praise God this week?

PRAY

Conclude the discussion with several minutes of fervent prayer for people in your circles of influence who have yet to experience the saving power of Jesus. Lift up these individuals as a group and pray for opportunities to share the gospel, your personal testimony, and your transformational testimony in the days to come.

GREAT COMMISSION WORSHIP IS MISSIONAL

There are several interesting buzzwords floating around Christian culture today.

Those words include *postmodern, authentic, organic, contextual, reformed,* and *community*. But a bigger buzzword has risen up in the past few years. The word is *missional*. *Missional* means we're called to be on mission with God, demonstrating and sharing the good news of Jesus in our everyday lives, wherever we go and in whatever we do. Ed Stetzer says the key to understanding this idea is first to realize that the age of Christendom is dead:

> "Christendom," that realm or time when Christianity was the assumed religion of the West, has come to an end. No longer is Christianity the "chaplain" to the broader culture. Until the last several years in the history of the United States, Christianity was thought to be the "American religion" even though it was not embraced by everyone or practiced with the devotion that committed Christians would like. It was once perceived as part of America's ethos.[1]

A major reason for this demise is that Christians have compartmentalized essential biblical teachings on worship, evangelism, and the Great Commission, viewing these calls as tasks to perform—as outward reflections of our faith—rather than components of our spiritual DNA. This is why our expressions of worship must be missional. We must see the mandates of worship and witness as natural expressions of Great Commission worship. When we love God with all our hearts, we're compelled to live on mission for Him. Over the next few days we'll examine specific ways God has called us to live missional lives and to be a missional church in a post-Christendom era.

DAY 1

UNDERSTANDING GOD'S MISSION

The evangelical church has experienced numerous pendulum swings from emphasis to emphasis over the past several decades. Although these emphases are truths outlined in Scripture, sometimes they can cause strife in the church. However, many times these shifts in emphasis provide essential occasions to assess how well we're glorifying God in specific areas of our lives.

All Christians and all churches are susceptible to distraction from fundamental principles in Scripture. We're imperfect people who make up imperfect churches living in an imperfect world. And Satan is constantly attacking the people of God in an attempt to make us lose our focus. Yet God's mission for His people has never changed. He's called us to accept the salvation He provides through His Son and to be on mission in the world, making Great Commission worshipers who will bring Him glory.

Do you feel that your church is focused more on accomplishing certain tasks or on glorifying God? Explain your answer.

What's one way you personally get distracted from glorifying God? Why do you think you lose this focus?

The word *missional* emphasizes that being on mission isn't an extraneous task or an activity we take on but a part of who we are as followers of Christ. It's a way of living the gospel so that we constantly show our love for and commitment to Jesus and remain ready to share the good news with others.

Although *missional* might be the new buzzword in Christian circles, the concept is far from new. The pendulum is simply swinging back to a focus on living every day as missional Great Commission worshipers. This isn't to say previous generations have failed to live missional lives, but in an ever-changing, post-Christian culture we need a fresh understanding of our biblical call to reach people.

Throughout the history of the church, our mission to deliver the gospel to the world has remained the same. Our mission should magnify and reflect the mission of God. This was true on the day of Pentecost, and it's true for us today as we seek to reach a lost world by the power of the Holy Spirit. These truths are clearly communicated in the pages of God's Word. Because of the unwavering, steadfast nature of God and His Word, we can maintain a clear, unapologetic view of our calling as Great Commission worshipers.

GOD IS ON MISSION

When we began this study, we looked at the Great Commandment and the Great Commission as expressions of Jesus' call for His followers to worship the Lord and to be on mission with Him:

> "Love the Lord your God with all your heart, with all your soul, and with all your mind." This is the greatest and most important command. The second is like it: "Love your neighbor as yourself." All the Law and the Prophets depend on these two commands.
>
> Matthew 22:37-40

> Jesus came near and said to them, "All authority has been given to Me in heaven and on earth. Go, therefore, and make disciples of all nations, baptizing them in the name of the Father and of the Son and of the Holy Spirit, teaching them to observe everything I have commanded you. And remember, I am with you always, to the end of the age."
>
> Matthew 28:18-20

Behind the Great Commission and the Great Commandment is the God who's communicated His saving purpose for all creation throughout His Word. As missional worshipers, we must understand that all Scripture can and should be read in light of God's desire for the nations to worship Him. Christopher Wright sheds light on this process, which he calls the missional hermeneutic. He explains:

A missional hermeneutic, then, is not content simply to call for obedience to the Great *Commission* (though it will assuredly include that as a matter of nonnegotiable importance), nor even to reflect on the missional implications of the Great *Commandment*. For behind both it will find [in the Bible] the Great *Communication*— the revelation of the identity of God, of God's action in the world and God's saving purpose for all creation.[2]

Wright argues that as the revelation of God, the entire Bible should be viewed through a missional lens of interpretation: "The Bible renders to us the story of God's mission through God's people in their engagement with God's world for the sake of the whole of God's creation."[3]

This radically challenges our approach to interpreting the Bible as it relates to God's missional work in history. If the whole Bible—Old and New Testaments— is to be interpreted in light of God's redeeming activity throughout history, it then becomes God's missionary journal to us, explaining how He's always been active in mobilizing His people for missional endeavors.[4]

Read the following verses and identify how they show God on mission through His people.

Genesis 12:1-3

Isaiah 49:6-7

1 John 4:9

How would seeing all Scripture as a record of God's redemptive work in history change the way you read the Word?

From Genesis to Revelation, God actively pursued fallen men and women, first to be redeemed and then to join Him on mission as Great Commission worshipers, proclaiming eternal hope to a lost world. This mandate has never changed.

ON MISSION WITH GOD

What does it actually mean to live missionally in the world? Is it enough just to love people and want them to come to Christ as we have? According to Ed Stetzer and Dave Putman in *Breaking the Missional Code,* "How we do mission flows from our understanding of God's mission."[5] But having an understanding or a missional heart is not enough. We must also establish a biblical foundation that directs and shapes our daily behavior as authentic servants of God. We must then accept God's invitation to participate in His mission in our neighborhoods, in our communities, and around the world.

Are you participating in God's redeeming mission? List ways you're engaged in God's mission and ways you can be more engaged.

Currently Engaged	Ways to Be More Engaged
1.	1.
2.	2.
3.	3.

Read Romans 10:13-15. How can you live on mission for God without ever leaving your ZIP code?

Joseph Aldrich wrote, "God's evangelistic strategy in a nutshell: He desires to build into you and me the beauty of his own character, and then put us on display."[6]

Name one way God has recently built His character in you.

Why is allowing God to shape and mold you into His likeness important in order to live missionally?

How does the gospel message propel you to be on mission for God?

Our focus as Great Commission worshipers should always be on the gospel and on our response to it. The gospel of Jesus Christ is not only truth to be understood but also a call for daily response in every area in our lives. We're to bear the gospel message in the context of our own place of influence and to creatively participate in God's redeeming work in history.

TODAY'S EVANGELISM EXPRESSION

As you continue this week of study, ask God to reveal areas of your life that need to be reenergized by the gospel. Ask Him to align your mission with His. As you read God's Word, look for God's redemptive purpose for all people and let it equip you to live on mission for Him.

TODAY'S WORSHIP EXPRESSION

Sing or read the following verse from the hymn "To Worship, Work, and Witness." It's sung to the tune of "Stand Up, Stand Up for Jesus." As you do, reflect on the truth of these words:

> To worship, work, and witness, the Good News spread abroad,
> We magnify thy mission, church of the living God;
> The Father's new creation thro' Jesus Christ his Son,
> The Spirit has empowered to do as Christ has done.[7]

DAY 2

PROCLAIMING THE WONDERS OF GOD

Is there a difference between believing in Jesus and following Jesus? And if so, what's that difference? Churches and believers are facing those questions today. And just as it's important to know how to answer them, it's even more important to know how to actively respond.

Actually, there's a huge gap between believing and following. When we fail to see that gap, we often develop calloused hearts and become ineffective ambassadors for the Kingdom. Whereas belief in Jesus can be embraced with no work or effort at all, following Jesus requires both belief and obedience. In other words, you can believe in Jesus while sitting on your couch with the remote clutched tightly in your hand, but following Jesus must happen outside the walls of your home and church. That's where Jesus is working to redeem and care for the lost.

Which category would you place yourself in: believer or follower? What evidence would make you answer that way?

How would you describe your current status as a follower of Christ?

❏ Diving   ❏ Reviving   ❏ Surviving   ❏ Thriving

Missional might be the biggest buzzword in our postmodern culture. But its intent and application to our daily living reach far past the novelty and triteness of language. This concept helps form and shape our vision, focus, and direction as Great Commission worshipers. William Temple once said:

> The world can be saved by one thing and that is worship. For to worship is to quicken the conscience by the holiness of God, to feed the mind with the truth of God, to purge the imagination by the beauty of God, to open the heart to the love of God, to devote the will to the purpose of God.[8]

Great Commission worship is missional. The intent of the Great Commission is to carry the gospel to a lost and dying world, proclaiming the wonders of God. That's the mission of every Great Commission worshiper.

TWO LEVELS OF MISSIONAL LIVING

Great Commission worshipers are missional on two levels.

1. Great Commission worshipers take the gospel to the nations. Great Commission worshipers seek to make disciples of Jesus by compelling people to become worshipers of the living Lord, sharing their faith, promoting His wonders, preaching the good news, and proclaiming the glory of God. Paul described our responsibility this way:

> We are ambassadors for Christ, certain that God is appealing through us. We plead on Christ's behalf, "Be reconciled to God."
>
> 2 Corinthians 5:20

2. Great Commission worshipers reach out to the needy, feed the hungry, care for the sick, embrace the marginalized, take in orphans, love widows, and accept the unwanted.

Jesus described His own ministry as a Servant:

> The Spirit of the Lord is on Me,
> because He has anointed Me
> to preach good news to the poor.
> He has sent Me
> to proclaim freedom to the captives
> and recovery of sight to the blind,
> to set free the oppressed,
> to proclaim the year of the Lord's favor.
>
> Luke 4:18-19

Jesus called His followers to be servants as well:

> Whoever wants to become great among you must be your servant.
>
> Mark 10:43

By serving others, we meet their needs in Jesus' name, and we gain opportunities to tell them the good news of Jesus.

Read the following verses and record our role as missional believers.

Proverbs 19:17

Galatians 5:14

James 1:27

Great Commission worshipers are Jesus' hands and feet to the world. We're driven by a passion for God and a deep love for others. We internalize the missional call of God with such conviction that it becomes our life's driving passion. And our obedience to that mission is driven by a deep love for Jesus.

Identify a time in the past six months when you surrendered yourself to serve someone else, not expecting anything in return.

What's prevented you from selflessly serving others in the past?

MISSIONAL LIVING KEEPS THE FOCUS ON GOD

God's redemptive purpose is evident throughout Scripture. And God's intent has always been to involve His people in missional endeavors that bring new worshipers to His throne. We see this in the act of creation, when God's intent was to establish a people who would glorify Him and live in a relationship of worship and freedom. We see it in God's call to Abraham, when He promised that "all the peoples on earth" would be blessed through Abraham and his descendants (Gen. 12:3).

Many great examples of this missional theme are found in the psalms. Psalm 96 is a great expression of God's heart for an unsaved world:

Sing a new song to the LORD;
sing to the LORD, all the earth.
Sing to Yahweh, praise His name;
proclaim His salvation from day to day.
Declare His glory among the nations,
His wonderful works among all peoples.
For the LORD is great and is highly praised;
He is feared above all gods.
For all the gods of the peoples are idols,
but the LORD made the heavens.
Splendor and majesty are before Him;
strength and beauty are in His sanctuary.
Ascribe to the LORD, you families of the peoples,
ascribe to the LORD glory and strength.
Ascribe to Yahweh the glory of His name;
bring an offering and enter His courts.
Worship the LORD in the splendor of His holiness;
tremble before Him, all the earth.
Say among the nations: "The LORD reigns.
The world is firmly established; it cannot be shaken.
He judges the peoples fairly."
Let the heavens be glad and the earth rejoice;
let the sea and all that fills it resound.
Let the fields and everything in them exult.
Then all the trees of the forest will shout for joy
before the LORD, for He is coming—
for He is coming to judge the earth.
He will judge the world with righteousness
and the peoples with His faithfulness.

List all of the things God has done or will do.

What are God's people called to do?

How do you see evangelism and worship coming together
in this psalm?

The psalmist called the people of Israel to join God's mission of proclaiming His redemption to all nations. In doing so, he gives us a glimpse of how God means for evangelism and worship to coexist.

The problem is that sometimes we're guilty of communicating the message of the gospel without considering the wonders of the One whose works we're proclaiming. Every time we proclaim His wonders through our witness to the world, it's a supreme act of missional worship and evangelism. Because the wonders of God are expressed through His people and mirrored in His creation, the nations can come to know and worship Him.

God's ultimate desire has never changed from the moment He spoke the world into existence. He wants His message of redemption to be spread to the nations, and He desires genuine worship from all people.

Describe the way your worship of God can lead you to share His message of salvation with those who need to hear it.

TODAY'S EVANGELISM EXPRESSION

Many Christians are busy with evangelism and ministry but never worship. Some sing songs and lift their hands but never share the gospel with their neighbors. A worshiping saint—someone who's completely fallen in love with Jesus and thoroughly understands the transformative power of worship—will always engage in evangelism. It's impossible for a person who worships in spirit and truth not to demonstrate the wonder of God in his or her life.

What does it mean for you, in your context, to be a missional follower of Christ?

TODAY'S WORSHIP EXPRESSION

Read aloud Psalm 108:1-6 and allow this to be your prayer to God. Write verses 5-6 on a piece of paper or on an index card and display it where it can remind you of your call to be on mission with God, proclaiming His wonders to the world.

DAY 3

JESUS' MISSIONAL MINISTRY

You've likely studied or heard about famous missions in United States history. Christopher Columbus's journey in 1492, for example, had an enormous impact on the historical development of the modern Western world. His perseverance through challenging voyages spoke volumes about his passion for discovery.

Lewis and Clark's expedition in the early 1800s to the Pacific Ocean was also very important scientifically, geographically, and economically for the United States. The Virginia-born explorers, commissioned by President Thomas Jefferson, discovered more than two hundred new plants and animals, documented at least 72 different Indian tribes, and recorded invaluable writings and maps.[9]

Perhaps Neil Armstrong and Buzz Aldrin undertook the most amazing mission in 1969. This mission, Apollo 11, took two men out of this world, into space, onto the face of the moon, and then back to Earth safely. This expedition, which opened the door for space exploration, was truly "one giant leap for mankind."

What other famous missions in United States history do you recall?

What makes these heroes so remarkable?

It's natural for us to appreciate a good mission. We all want to be a part of something much bigger than what our ordinary lives offer. As Great Commission worshipers, we have an opportunity to be on mission. But this is a divine mission—God's mission. And although Jesus Christ has already accomplished this mission, it continues today through His people.

SENT

In the Gospel of John alone you'll find about 60 instances where the word *sent, send,* or *sending* is used. A majority of those times, about 40, are the words of Jesus, which refer to His being sent by the Father.

After Jesus' resurrection His disciples gathered behind locked doors, fearing the Jewish leaders who had crucified Him. Suddenly Jesus appeared and greeted them: "Peace to you!" (John 20:19). He showed them His wounds, and they rejoiced to see that He was alive. Then He commissioned them to continue His ministry on earth: "As the Father has sent Me, I also send you" (v. 21).

Why were these words important for the disciples to hear?

In regard to the Great Commission, why is it important for believers to understand that Jesus was sent by the Father?

Just as the Father sent Jesus, Jesus sends us. He sends us into the world to do what He did: spread the gospel and make disciples. David Hesselgrave, in his book *Paradigms in Conflict*, describes Jesus' example:

> By fulfilling his mission in this way, Jesus modeled attitudes, lifestyle, activities, and methods that are worth emulating in missions ministry today. Missions and missionaries should think as he thought, say what he said, and do what he did. In doing so, they continue his ministry.[10]

Jesus is our model for carrying out our Father's redemptive mission. If we aren't going on mission every day, we aren't being obedient to the One who's gone before us and who's called us to go and make disciples.

Describe what Jesus has sent you to do in your world.

OUR MISSIONAL MODEL

The New Testament provides numerous examples of Jesus' serving as a model of missional living. The account of the woman at the well perfectly illustrates Jesus' missional lifestyle, which uniquely combined both worship and evangelism.

Read John 4:4-12. What are your initial observations about this encounter?

How do you see Jesus' compassion in this passage?

Jesus' character and compassion are evident in the way He treated this woman. Several small details verify His missional commitment to reach out to the unloved and disregarded in His culture. One is the fact that Jesus intentionally traveled through Samaria even though many Jews would have never risked the possibility of mingling with the despised half-breeds. Keep in mind that the Jews didn't merely dislike the Samaritans; they viewed them as impure and unworthy of God's mercy or their attention.

The actions of Christ should compel the church to intentionally engage with cultural Samaritans—the unloved people and outcasts we meet in our everyday lives who need to hear the good news. As Jesus stated in Matthew 25:40, "I assure you: Whatever you did for one of the least of these brothers of Mine, you did for Me." Missional worshipers are always concerned with the needs of hurting people.

Have you ever intentionally interacted with an outcast in society? If so, briefly describe your experience. If not, why not?

How would you characterize your sensitivity to the needs of others? Why?

❐ Compassionate   ❐ When convenient
❐ Mostly distracted   ❐ Blind

To the average Jewish male, the woman represented two things he looked down on most: a Samaritan and an adulterer. But Jesus saw this woman in a different light. To Him, she was much more than a social outcast. And Jesus' simple yet powerful words "Give Me a drink" (John 4:7) confirmed that He was conscious of being on mission with the Father and was therefore attentive to her needs.

Jesus' interaction with the Samaritan woman demonstrates two ways He serves as our missional model.

1. Jesus' words affirmed the woman's humanity and her value to God. Jesus helped her recognize who she really was to God the Father. Contrary to Jewish practices, Jesus confirmed that this Samaritan woman mattered to God and deserved Jesus' attention, His mercy, and the opportunity for salvation.

2. Jesus obviously cared more about the woman's soul than religious traditions. Because of His missional DNA, He was willing to converse with a known adulterer and sinner.

How can religious traditions take precedence over biblical truth and prevent churches from going on mission to their communities?

How have religious traditions prevented you from following Jesus' missional model?

Jesus further addressed the woman's sin and His real identity.

Read John 4:13-26. How did Jesus confront the woman about her sin?

Jesus was intentional yet patient to carefully engage the woman in truth. He knew the woman must first be confronted with her sin before He could discuss her need of salvation. Jesus accomplished this by addressing the issue of her five husbands and her adulterous lifestyle. Notice that Jesus established a rapport with the woman before confronting her sin.

In a relational culture like ours, most people won't receive the truth until they first see it demonstrated in other believers. Missional worshipers must therefore be genuine and real.

How would you describe genuine worship, based on Jesus' words in verses 21-24?

Jesus then called for the woman to submit her life to the lordship of the Father, worshiping Him in "spirit and truth" (v. 23). A proper understanding of worship always involves complete submission and surrender.

Look at the effects of the woman's response in verses 39-42:

> Many Samaritans from that town believed in Him because of what the woman said when she testified, "He told me everything I ever did." Therefore, when the Samaritans came to Him, they asked Him to stay with them, and He stayed there two days. Many more believed because of what He said. And they told the woman, "We no longer believe because of what you said, for we have heard for ourselves and know that this really is the Savior of the world."

This adulterous Samaritan woman was not only hated by the Jews but was also an outcast in her own society. Yet once she understood Jesus' true identity, she was compelled to worship Him in total obedience, proclaiming His message and inviting the whole city to come and meet the Messiah.

How do you see worship and evangelism working together in Jesus' encounter with the Samaritan woman?

How can Jesus' example change the way you approach witnessing?

Regardless of religious traditions we might follow and personal prejudices we might harbor, we should always be careful not to limit God's grace and mercy to a certain segment of society or culture.

Our mission to carry the gospel to a lost and dying world is the intent of the Great Commission, but at the heart of the Great Commission is worship of Jesus. The Holy Spirit equips, fills, energizes, and empowers worshipers to declare God's wonders to unbelievers. Therefore, worship is missional. When God's people truly fall in love with Christ, they will live missional lives. They can't be silent about His grace and mercy.

Identify outcasts or unloved people in your community. What would it take to show them the love of Jesus?

TODAY'S WORSHIP EXPRESSION

Set an alarm throughout the day to remind you to stop and reflect on what Christ accomplished on the cross. Praise God during those times for the missional model He sent us in Christ.

DAY 4

THE CHURCH ON MISSION

Seeing or hearing the word *Coke®* should immediately conjure all kinds of images, tastes, and sounds in your head. You probably imagine the logo, the classic glass bottle, and a polar bear or Santa Claus drinking the ice-cold drink at Christmastime. You might also hear the familiar jingles, taste the sweet syrup, and feel the fizz at the back of your throat. All from one word.

It's no surprise that the Coca-Cola® Company is the most recognized company in the world. It's documented that *Coca-Cola* is the second most understood term in the world after *OK*. Research has also shown that 94 percent of the world's population recognizes the red and white Coca-Cola logo. Altogether about 1.7 billion servings of Coca-Cola products are guzzled down every day.

Why is Coca-Cola so recognized? It might be because the company spends about three billion dollars a year on advertising, more than Microsoft® and Apple® combined.[11] It might also be due to the long-standing reputation and brand loyalty that have steadily grown since the company started in downtown Atlanta in 1886. Whatever the reason, Coca-Cola has successfully communicated its message and has made itself known in the world.

What are other brands or companies that have worldwide recognition? In your opinion, what's the secret to their success?

Imagine a world where every nation, every people group, and every neighbor recognized the name of Jesus. Imagine a world where people all around us were moving from death to life in Jesus. Imagine a world where every church emphasized missional living and sent their people into their communities and throughout the world to proclaim the name of Jesus. That's exactly what we're called to do as Great Commission worshipers. And unlike Coca-Cola, our message quenches a thirst that nothing else can satisfy.

THE CHURCH DOESN'T EXIST FOR ITSELF

We often think of the church as an organization made up of teachers, lawyers, doctors, students, auto mechanics, and farmers. But this way of thinking pushes our focus inward instead of outward. We should think of the church as believers on mission for God, being sent out as teachers, lawyers, doctors, students, auto mechanics, and farmers. It's not enough to merely be concerned with the world around us or to be mission-minded. We're to be salt and light in the world, permeating society with Jesus' character and message of hope. Therefore, "let your light shine before men, so that they may see your good works and give glory to your Father in heaven" (Matt. 5:16).

Ed Stetzer identifies the difference between a church that's mission-minded and one that's missional. He explains:

> Don't confuse the terms *mission-minded* and *missional*. The first refers more to an attitude of *caring* about missions, particularly overseas. *Missional* means actually *doing mission* right where you are. *Missional* means adopting the *posture of a missionary*, learning and adapting to the culture around you while remaining biblically sound. Think of it this way: *missional* means being a missionary without ever leaving your zip code.[12]

He goes on further to explain that a missional church is called to go on mission with Christ. This simply means "being intentional and deliberate about reaching others."[13] This doesn't mean, however, that being missional is about merely "putting more time into trying to reach out to the neighborhood."[14] Rather, "being missional begins with a profound conviction that we are invited to join in the mission of God and that the church does not exist for itself, but rather for the world around us that God so desperately loves."[15]

List opportunities your church provides to reach out to the community. How are you involved in these?

What are some ways a church as a whole can live missionally in the world that would be difficult to do on your own?

THE CONTEXTUAL CHURCH

In Acts 2 the church was born when the Holy Spirit was revealed in power at Pentecost. As a result, Peter preached a message of repentance, and three thousand people responded in faith. Almost immediately, the new believers adopted a missional mind-set of community, worship, and lifestyle evangelism:

> They devoted themselves to the apostles' teaching, to the fellowship, to the breaking of bread, and to the prayers. Then fear came over everyone, and many wonders and signs were being performed through the apostles. Now all the believers were together and held all things in common. They sold their possessions and property and distributed the proceeds to all, as anyone had a need. Every day they devoted themselves to meeting together in the temple complex, and broke bread from house to house. They ate their food with a joyful and humble attitude, praising God and having favor with all the people. And every day the Lord added to them those who were being saved.
>
> Acts 2:42-47

How is that description similar to your church? How is it different?

Unlike many churches today, the church in Acts didn't try to attract people to a location to hear the gospel. The early believers understood the power of an incarnational witness, personally embodying the message of Christ by representing Him in a spirit of humility, worship, and unity. They understood that worship and evangelism are more than religious practices, as the Jews of that day had come to see them. Their missional authenticity was undeniable, opening the door for them to proclaim the wonders of Christ.

How does a church begin to see worship and evangelism merely as religious duties?

How can a church keep that from happening?

The early believers didn't remain behind closed doors. They took the good news of Jesus into their community. This was the beginning of the contextual church, a church that understands the needs of the surrounding community, personally engages with unbelievers in their context through an incarnational witness, and intentionally demonstrates and shares the message of Christ.

How would you characterize your church's cultural context?

How is your church specifically engaging with people in that context?

A church seeking to be on mission with God in its context must ask important missional questions:
• How are we engaging culture where people are?
• How are we ministering to the unchurched, not just the already churched?
• How are we compelled by the gospel to seek and serve the hurting and the unloved?
• If our church were gone tomorrow, would those outside the church miss our presence?

How would you answer those questions on behalf of your church?

A contextual church shouldn't be a cultural chameleon, so enmeshed with its surroundings that it can no longer be recognized as the body of Christ. But we should connect and interact with our community in a very genuine, authentic way. A contextual church loves, ministers to, and serves people where they are in order to engage them with the gospel.

TODAY'S EVANGELISM EXPRESSION

Think specifically about the needs of unbelievers you committed last week to pray for. How can you or your church serve them by meeting their physical, emotional, and spiritual needs? Write their names and beside each one identify a need and one way it can be met.

TODAY'S WORSHIP EXPRESSION

Read George Peters's definition of the word *mission:*

> *Mission*, in my usage, refers to the total biblical assignment of the church of Jesus Christ. It is a comprehensive term including the upward, inward and outward ministries of the church. It is the church as "sent" ... in this world.[16]

Reflect on ways you and your church have responded to being sent into the world. Pray that God will use your church to bring people to Himself.

DAY 5

TO GLORIFY GOD

You might have heard the Latin term *missio dei,* translated as *the mission of God.* This is essentially what we've been talking about all week: what God's mission is and how we can be a part of it. Today let's dig a little deeper, looking at a central element at play in the *missio dei.*

Is going on mission with God about evangelism? Yes, but it's more than that. Evangelism isn't the ultimate goal of our participation in the *missio dei.* Instead, evangelism is the means to an end. That end is to glorify Almighty God.

D. Martyn Lloyd-Jones wrote, "The supreme object of the work of evangelism is to glorify God, *not* to save souls. … The only power that can do this work is the Holy Spirit, *not* our own strength."[17] Therefore, God will bring glory to Himself by redeeming a lost world. And we can be God's instruments to bring Him glory by intentionally joining His redemptive work.

What's your reaction to the idea that glorifying God, not evangelism, is the ultimate goal of being on mission with God?

How does this idea change your perspective on living a missional life?

With this new idea in mind, let's step back and take a big-picture look at a Great Commission worshiper and the importance of seeking the right goal.

A MISSIONAL WORSHIPER

Yesterday we saw that the church doesn't exist for itself but for the world around us, whom God loves and sent His Son to die for. Being missional is living daily an authentic and intentional life of worship that embodies the ministry passion of Christ. In short, it means becoming a sold-out Great Commission worshiper. Worship, therefore, has a critical connection to becoming a missional Christian.

Why would it be unbiblical to worship God without also sharing the good news of salvation?

We can't passionately pursue the heartbeat of God through worship while knowingly disobeying Him in regard to being on mission. Obedience to God is the core value of biblical worship. If we disobey Him in the temporal area of evangelism, we'll lose the very thing we're pursuing—authentic worship. It's impossible to truly worship in spirit and truth while failing to demonstrate the wonders of God in our lives by going on mission.

Worship, therefore, motivates believers to become authentic evangelists. John Piper says, "Worship is the fuel and the goal of missions."[18]

How is worship the fuel and goal of missions?

Which do you tend to neglect more—evangelism or worship? How does that affect your efforts to bring glory to God?

In no way should we ignore God's call to be involved in the Great Commission. It's our call to worship. The immediate necessity is to proclaim the gospel until the day Christ returns and every true believer is ushered into God's presence in heaven. At that point there will no longer be a need for evangelism, and we'll worship eternally. Until then we must do as Christ commands and passionately embrace our missional calling to spread the gospel to the ends of the earth.

A MISSIONAL SERVANT

According to Van Sanders, God's design for the mission of His people *"is to be His instrument through which He creates one, called out, holy people for His glory and worship from all peoples of the world."*[19] Paul also used the word *instruments* in Romans 6:13: "Present yourselves to God as those who have been brought from death to life, and your members to God as instruments for righteousness" (ESV). One practical way we can be God's instruments is to serve unbelievers.

Jesus saw Himself as a Servant of His Father and of all humankind. He said, "The Son of Man did not come to be served, but to serve, and to give His life—a ransom for many" (Matt. 20:28). By serving, Jesus brought glory to God and provided the way people could be saved. Jesus also taught His disciples to be servants. After washing His disciples' feet, He said, "I have given you an example that you also should do just as I have done for you" (John 13:15).

Describe times when you've served a believer and an unbeliever.

Believer:

Unbeliever:

How can serving an unbeliever lead to evangelism?

Being on mission requires living an incarnational lifestyle. Just as Jesus left heaven and lived missionally among us to glorify God, He calls us to live missionally in our culture for the same purpose. When we serve unbelievers, we incarnate the gospel with our very lives. Service often opens doors to an evangelistic witness. It also visibly demonstrates the love, compassion, and hope we offer with our words.

A missional believer serves as an involuntary compulsion. Don't serve because it's your duty. Serve because you can't resist serving. Loving others through authentic service is an essential component of Great Commission worship.

TODAY'S EVANGELISM EXPRESSION

This week commit yourself to serving others, not with the intent of receiving any acknowledgment or glory of your own but with the intent of glorifying God.

Take the prayer list you've been using and read the needs of those you've been praying for, both believers and unbelievers. Start meeting their needs through Christlike service. This service can take many forms. If the person on your prayer list is a neighbor, surprise them by mowing their yard or by cooking a meal for them. You could also volunteer to babysit or simply begin asking these neighbors if they have prayer needs.

Go through your list one by one and ask God to receive glory as you serve the people you're praying for. Ask Him to give you an opportunity through your service to demonstrate and verbalize the gospel.

TODAY'S WORSHIP EXPRESSION

Take a moment to thank God that He's invited you to be on mission with Him. Praise Him that salvation doesn't come from your own ability or power but from the One who's able and omnipotent. Ask God to show you ways you're failing to give Him all glory.

1. Ed Stetzer, *Planting Missional Churches* (Nashville: B&H, 2006), 19.
2. Christopher J. H. Wright, *The Mission of God* (Downers Grove, IL: InterVarsity, 2006), 60.
3. Ibid., 22.
4. Alvin Reid, *Evangelism Handbook* (Nashville: B&H, 2009), 48.
5. Ed Stetzer and David Putman, *Breaking the Missional Code* (Nashville: B&H, 2006), 53.
6. Joseph Aldrich, in Robert J. Morgan, *Nelson's Complete Book of Stories, Illustrations, and Quotes* (Nashville: Thomas Nelson, 2000), 777.
7. Henry Lyle Lambdin, "To Worship, Work, and Witness," *Baptist Hymnal* (Nashville: Convention Press, 1975), 238.
8. William Temple, in Morgan, *Nelson's Complete Book,* 808.
9. Jack Uldrich, *Into the Unknown* (New York: American Management Association, 2004), 37.
10. David J. Hesselgrave, *Paradigms in Conflict* (Grand Rapids: Kregel, 2005), 150.
11. Kim Bhasin, "15 Facts About Coca-Cola That Will Blow Your Mind," *Business Insider* [online], 9 June 2011 [cited 17 October 2012]. Available from the Internet: *www.businessinsider.com.*
12. Stetzer, *Planting Missional Churches,* 19.
13. Ibid.
14. Cam Roxburgh, in *Discipling Our Nation,* ed. Murray Moerman (Delta, BC Canada: Church Leadership Library, 2005), 151, as quoted in John M. Bailey, "The Missional Church," in *Pursuing the Mission of God in Church Planting,* comp. John M. Bailey (Alpharetta, GA: North American Mission Board, 2006), 39.
15. Ibid.
16. George W. Peters, *A Biblical Theology of Missions* (Chicago: Moody Bible Institute, 1972).
17. D. Martyn Lloyd-Jones, in Will McRaney, *The Art of Personal Evangelism* (Nashville: B&H, 2003), 49.
18. John Piper, *Let the Nations Be Glad,* 3d ed. (Grand Rapids: Baker, 2010), 255.
19. Van Sanders, "The Mission of God and the Local Church," in Bailey, comp., *Pursuing the Mission of God in Church Planting,* 15–16.

WEEK 4 GROUP EXPERIENCE

Use the following activity to introduce the topics covered in this week's study.

SUPPLIES NEEDED. Consider using a chalkboard, a whiteboard, or a large sheet of paper, along with appropriate writing implements.

ACTIVITY. As a group, identify several missions that have had the most impact on modern culture in recent decades. For example, those who were alive in 1969 might list the Apollo 11 mission to the moon. These missions can be military, exploratory, scientific, evangelistic, and so on. After spending three or four minutes preparing a list of missions, discuss the following questions.

Which mission had the greatest impact on you personally? Why?

Which of these missions evokes the strongest emotional reaction in you? What emotions are you experiencing?

In your own words, how would you describe the mission we're currently engaged in as followers of Christ?

Prepare for further group discussion by reading aloud the following passage.

> The Spirit of the Lord is on Me,
> because He has anointed Me
> to preach good news to the poor.
> He has sent Me
> to proclaim freedom to the captives
> and recovery of sight to the blind,
> to set free the oppressed,
> to proclaim the year of the Lord's favor.
>
> Luke 4:18-19

Use the following excerpts from the study material to move below the surface and engage in transformational conversations.

DAY 1. The word *missional* refers to our call to be on mission with God to demonstrate and share the good news of Jesus in our everyday lives, wherever we go and in whatever we do. It emphasizes that being on mission with God isn't an extraneous task or an activity we take on but a part of who we are as followers of Christ. It's a way of living the gospel so that we constantly show our love for and commitment to Jesus and remain ready to share the good news with others.

What images or ideas come to mind when you hear the word *missional*? Why?

How does the gospel message propel you to be on mission for God?

DAY 2. Great Commission worshipers are Jesus' hands and feet to the world. We're driven by a passion for God and a deep love for others. We internalize the missional call of God with such conviction that it becomes our life's driving passion. And our obedience to that mission is driven by a deep love for Jesus.

What opportunities have you recently had to serve others?

How has your relationship with Jesus motivated you to live the Christian life well? How has it motivated you to serve others?

What obstacles have prevented or discouraged you from serving others in the past?

DAY 3. The New Testament provides numerous examples of Jesus' serving as a model of missional living. The account of the woman at the well perfectly illustrates Jesus' missional lifestyle, which uniquely combined both worship and evangelism.

Read John 4:4-12. What are your initial observations about this encounter?

How do you see Jesus' compassion in this passage?

This adulterous Samaritan woman was not only hated by the Jews but was also an outcast in her own society. Yet once she understood Jesus' true identity, she was compelled to worship Him in total obedience, proclaiming His message and inviting the whole city to come and meet the Messiah.

How do you see worship and evangelism working together in Jesus' encounter with the Samaritan woman?

DAY 4. Imagine a world where every nation, every people group, and every neighbor recognized the name of Jesus. Imagine a world where people all around us were moving from death to life in Jesus. Imagine a world where every church emphasized missional living and sent their people into their communities and throughout the world to proclaim the name of Jesus. That's exactly what we're called to do as Great Commission worshipers.

What emotions do you experience when you hear these words? Why?

The early believers didn't remain behind closed doors. They took the good news of Jesus into their community. This was the beginning of the contextual church, a church that understands the needs of the surrounding community, personally engages with unbelievers in their context through an incarnational witness, and intentionally demonstrates and shares the message of Christ.

How would you characterize your church's cultural context?

How is your church specifically engaging with people in that context?

DAY 5. We can't passionately pursue the heartbeat of God through worship and knowingly disobey Him in regard to being on mission. Obedience to God is the core value of biblical worship. If we disobey Him in the temporal area of evangelism, we'll lose the very thing we're pursuing—authentic worship. It's impossible to truly worship in spirit and truth while failing to demonstrate the wonders of God in our lives by going on mission.

Worship, therefore, motivates believers to become authentic evangelists.

Which do you tend to neglect more—evangelism or worship?

How does that affect your efforts to bring glory to God?

APPLY TO LIFE

Discuss your experiences with the Evangelism Expression and Worship Expression at the end of each day's study material.

What are you most looking forward to in your future efforts to serve the needs of others? Why?

What makes you the most nervous or fearful about those future efforts? Why?

The Worship Expression at the end of day 2 challenged you to display Psalm 108:5-6 where you could see it regularly. Read those verses aloud and talk about the impact of that challenge.

PRAY

Conclude this group discussion with a prayer of intercession for your community. Speak with God about specific needs you're aware of, both in your church and in the larger sphere of life around your church. Speak with God about people who are suffering physically, emotionally, financially, and especially spiritually. Ask for Him to work in the midst of those needs. Ask God to give your group members opportunities to be on mission.

GREAT COMMISSION WORSHIP IS REPRODUCIBLE

This week we come to the final element of Great Commission worship.

The natural progression in becoming a Great Commission worshiper is to reproduce other worshipers by going and making disciples. Walter Henrichsen illustrates this principle in *Disciples Are Made, Not Born:*

> Some time ago there was a display at the Museum of Science and Industry in Chicago. It featured a checkerboard with 1 grain of wheat on the first, 2 on the second, 4 on the third, then 8, 16, 32, 64, 128, etc. Somewhere down the board, there were so many grains of wheat on the square that some were spilling over into neighboring squares—so here the demonstration stopped. Above the checkerboard display was a question, "At this rate of doubling every square, how much grain would be on the checkerboards by the 64th square?" To find the answer to this riddle, you punched a button on the console in front of you, and the answer flashed on a little screen above the board: "Enough to cover the entire subcontinent of India 50 feet deep." Multiplication may be costly and, in the initial stages, much slower than addition, but in the long run, it is the most effective way of accomplishing Christ's Great Commission and the only way.[1]

An intentional process of reproduction is essential to complete the cycle of biblical discipleship. When this process of multiplication occurs, a Great Commission worshiper is born.

DAY 1

A DISCIPLE MAKER

Jesus said, "Go, therefore, and make disciples of all nations, … teaching them to observe everything I have commanded you" (Matt. 28:19-20). We often get hung up with the last part of the Great Commission. We're fine with going, but we'd rather leave the teaching to the pastor or Sunday School teacher. The problem is that we can't make disciples by simply going.

A disciple is someone who follows Christ. So seeing someone acknowledge and believe Jesus died in their place for the forgiveness of their sins isn't enough. We must make disciples by teaching them how to follow Christ.

This is the most overlooked and underappreciated element of Great Commission worship. Someone can be submitting to God's formational and transformational work and living a relational and missional life but still fall short of Great Commission worship if they don't understand what it means to reproduce by making disciples.

When you were a new believer, who helped you know what it means to follow Christ?

What happens when churches stop after being missional, choosing not to teach new converts what it means to be followers of Christ?

The mandate of the Great Commission is to go into all the world and make fully devoted followers of Christ. The command to make disciples puts feet to the missional aspect of Great Commission worship. We live out the message of Christ in our daily routine of evangelism and worship. We communicate the Word of God by the way we live. We become part of the transformational process as we teach, train, develop, and nurture new worshipers. In these ways Great Commission worshipers reproduce followers of Jesus.

Unfortunately, the process of discipleship has consistently been misinterpreted and misapplied in most Christian circles. Rather than creating zealous followers of Christ who feel compelled to reproduce by joining Him on mission and by intentionally building relationships with unbelievers, contemporary discipleship is often limited to merely attending weekly classes through the church or meeting in small groups, with little or no expectation of representing Christ to the world.

Because this type of anemic discipleship doesn't reproduce Christ followers, it's detrimental to the Great Commission and hinders the spirit of reproduction.

MOBILIZED VS. EDUCATED BELIEVERS

The common belief among most Christians and many church leaders is that believers must achieve a high level of biblical and practical knowledge before they can become reproducing followers of Christ. Therefore, many believers, even those who've been born again for several years, feel unprepared to join Christ on mission as reproducing disciples; they think they aren't educated enough.

What factors have kept you from sharing your faith in the past?

☐ Fear   ☐ Disinterest
☐ Lack of knowledge   ☐ Few relationships
                                with lost people

The most common excuses for not sharing Jesus are a fear of rejection and a false belief that without experience and knowledge, the witness can't be effective. Nothing could be further from the truth. Consider the approach Jesus used with His disciples in Matthew 10:16-20:

> Look, I'm sending you out like sheep among wolves. Therefore be as shrewd as serpents and as harmless as doves. Because people will hand you over to sanhedrins and flog you in their synagogues, beware of them. You will even be brought before governors and kings because of Me, to bear witness to them and to the nations. But when they hand you over, don't worry about how or what you should speak. For you will be given what to say at that hour, because you are not speaking, but the Spirit of your Father is speaking through you.

When Jesus said, "Don't worry about how or what you should speak" (v. 19), does that sound as though the disciples needed great knowledge to reach unbelievers? Does it appear the disciples had passed all of their exams at the Jesus Institute of Biblical Studies before being deployed into the harvest? No.

On the contrary, Jesus simply instructed the disciples that they "will be given what to say at that hour" (v. 19). Even after spending countless hours at the feet of Jesus, the disciples still needed to depend on the Holy Spirit—just like us. So which comes first—education about discipleship or mobilization for making disciples? According to the example of Jesus, the correct answer is both.

What's your reaction to the previous statement? Why?

List three advantages that education and mobilization give Great Commission worshipers.

Education	Mobilization
1.	1.
2.	2.
3.	3.

DISCIPLESHIP ON THE GO

Making disciples starts with a deeper understanding of the process of discipleship. But people can't be properly trained as disciples unless they're placed in real-life situations that force them to overcome their fears and desire to grow spiritually. Jesus didn't educate the disciples in a classroom and then mobilize them into the field after they graduated with a seminary degree in evangelism or worship.

The disciples' primary qualifications to make new disciples were their personal experiences with Jesus. They went out on the mission field along with Him as He taught, healed, and preached. Those experiences effectively transformed the disciples into worshipers who reproduced themselves by sharing the gospel with unbelievers and discipling those who became believers.

Have your discipleship experiences majored more on education in the classroom or on moving out to make new disciples? How effectively have you made disciples this way?

Jesus sent the disciples out "like sheep among wolves" (v. 16). It appears Jesus viewed evangelism as the perfect process to achieve mature discipleship among His ragtag followers. He knew the disciples would face a myriad of theological issues. They would be challenged, attacked, wounded, and possibly killed. Yet Jesus still sent them out to proclaim the message of hope because He expected them to reproduce. He had limited earthly time with His disciples, so His main pursuit was to create a movement that would glorify His Father and spread the gospel around the globe. You and I have a part to play in that movement by multiplying Great Commission worshipers today.

TODAY'S EVANGELISM EXPRESSION

Think about ways you've discipled or are discipling someone as you answer the following questions.
- In your own words what does it mean to say Great Commission worship is reproducible?
- What's the difference between mobilization and education, and how does each impact the way believers and churches disciple new Christians?

TODAY'S WORSHIP EXPRESSION

As you continue this week's lessons, ask God to open your eyes to recognize your level of obedience in reproducing yourself in a lost world. Thank Him for the people He's put in your life who've guided you to become a follower of Christ.

DAY 2

A REPRODUCING WITNESS

Yesterday we observed that a discipleship process that depends on education alone without simultaneous, consistent mobilization into the harvest fields may result in apathetic worshipers who are indifferent to the urgency of the Great Commission.

There's no doubt that a spirit of indifference is killing the church. Many church members don't care about making disciples. Scripture describes this attitude as being lukewarm (see Rev. 3:16). It's been said that the opposite of love isn't hate; it's indifference. At least hate is motivated by passion. Apathy doesn't care enough to love. This attitude is gradually leading the church to remove itself from culture.

Today indifference has become the norm for many congregations. Rather than embracing people's needs, we choose to remain removed from the frontlines of ministry. This attitude affects the way the church does discipleship. Instead of engaging with the world to meet needs and share Christ's love, the church remains aloof, focuses on its own needs, and criticizes the world for acting sinful.

If your church were removed from your city, would anybody notice? Why or why not? What specific qualities and practices make your church an expression of Christ in your community?

REPRESENTING CHRIST IN THE WORLD

It seems that the church not only accepts indifference but also promotes it as normal behavior. John Avant explains this attitude of indifference this way:

The whole world has changed around us. Every church sits in the middle of a mission field. The diversity of races, cultures, religions, philosophies, and worldviews has grown so rapidly that it's shocking. You live on the mission field, but the truth is that most of Christianity is not terribly interested in Jesus' mission. Fulfilling that mission would require so much change from the current club regulations that one thing becomes clear to the doorkeepers: if they let this change in, the club will never be the same. It will not even resemble what it has been, and that's just too much to bear. So we appoint a professional class of missionaries to do the dirty work for us—and we make sure that the dirty work they do stays far enough from the front doors of our church buildings to avoid the nasty reminders that we ourselves are supposed to be doing something on this mission. We either celebrate the missionaries as distant heroes or, just as often, forget that they're even out there at all. Either way, we're free of the burden.[2]

This attitude of selfish indifference is deadly for the development of reproducing, Great Commission worshipers. Some church members move through life with little regard for the needs of hurting people. Their concept of worship and evangelism is limited to the church building on Sunday morning. They're conditioned to be indifferent because they lack biblical discipleship that challenges them to reproduce their faith. They believe ministry is the responsibility of paid staff members, not of everyday Christians. They're loyal to the institution of the church as long as it doesn't interfere with their daily lives.

In contrast, Jesus called us to be reproducing disciples. Recall Jesus' words to His disciples when He appeared after the resurrection: "As the Father has sent Me, I also send you" (John 20:21). Just as Jesus called the disciples to move out from behind the locked doors of the upper room, He calls His church to go into the world to represent Him and share His message. The apostle John described believers' presence in the world as an extension of God's love:

God is love. Whoever lives in love lives in God, and God in him. In this way, love is made complete among us so that we will have confidence on the day of judgment, because in this world we are like him.

1 John 4:16-17, NIV

What are some ways believers represent Jesus in the world?

Great Commission worshipers go on mission with God in their daily lives, lovingly engaging with the community, meeting human needs in the name of Christ, and sharing the message of salvation.

LINEAR VS. CYCLICAL DISCIPLESHIP

Yesterday we saw that education alone doesn't create reproducing disciples. Another misunderstanding in today's church is the fallacy of linear discipleship. This concept grows from the idea that true worshipers are created through a discipleship process that emphasizes a lifetime of intense training, usually in a protected environment like the church building.

Unfortunately, as evidenced by most Christians' anemic evangelistic practices, the result is a generation of believers who pursue biblical knowledge without the expectation of joining Christ on mission "to seek and to save the lost" (Luke 19:10). And regrettably, this linear approach has become the accepted process of discipleship in many Christian circles, where evangelism is often presented as a watered-down suggestion rather than a command.

Do you believe today's churches treat evangelism as a suggestion or a command for Christians? Why?

Have your actions in recent months supported what you believe about evangelism?

In contrast to linear discipleship is the biblical concept of cyclical discipleship. In this model when people respond to the gospel and are genuinely born again, they're immediately connected to the process of becoming a reproducing disciple. Because disciples are called to reproduce more disciples, evangelism and discipleship depend on each other. Therefore, evangelism is much more than sharing gospel presentations and seeking decisions. Discipleship is more than simply training people to memorize Bible verses. Neither the process of evangelism nor the process of discipleship is complete unless it intentionally meshes with the goal of leading the person who's evangelized to become a reproducing worshiper.

Reread Matthew 10:16-20. In what ways would Jesus' approach multiply believers?

Do you think your church tends to practice linear or cyclical discipleship? Explain your answer.

John Avant states:

> If we really believed God, everyone would be on the mission. In fact, I believe that the mission would be the very core of the church's DNA. No follower of Christ would be able to make any sense out of life lived apart from the mission of loving, serving, and sharing the good news with those who are not yet followers of Christ.[3]

Reproducing disciples don't have to be prodded by a pastor or church leader to be involved in ministry. They have a keen understanding that the church isn't a building or a location but the people of God. Reproducing disciples understand their faith to be an expression of what it means to be a follower of Christ. Evangelism and worship, therefore, are callings to be lived out and reproduced through their daily routines. And ultimately, real worshipers are motivated by obedience rather than duty.

Does your life match the description in the previous paragraph? Why or why not?

What are immediate actions you could take to become a reproducing disciple?

Paul envisioned a reproducing discipleship process when he counseled and taught the early churches.

Read 2 Timothy 2:1-3. What three commands did Paul give?

1.

2.

3.

Paul taught his young protégé Timothy that Great Commission worship is reproducible. Paul discipled Timothy, who would teach "faithful men." Those men would "teach others also" (v. 2). Our goal as reproducing disciples today is the same: to promote and bring into the body of Christ citizens from every tribe, tongue, culture, nation, and people group so that they can become worshipers too. The principles of 2 Timothy and our role as worshiping evangelists are tied to our responsibility to make disciples.

As a reproducible worshiper, you're responsible for exercising spiritual influence over the lives of those who need to become Great Commission worshipers or who need to be discipled. Through the power of the Holy Spirit, you can make an eternal difference in the lives of other people.

TODAY'S EVANGELISM EXPRESSION

Focus on ways you and your church express Christ's presence in the world as His followers. Start thinking about ways you can more effectively represent God's mission through your worship and witness.

TODAY'S WORSHIP EXPRESSION

Meditate on 1 John 4:16-17. How often do you thank God for His love and express your love to Him in praise? How does His love motivate you to represent Jesus as you go about your daily life? How does His love push you to reach out to people with compassion and urgency? Pray that your love for others will reflect God's love for you.

DAY 3

THE GOSPEL WE SHARE

We've learned in this study that a Great Commission worshiper should do everything from a love for God and a love for others. That's Jesus' message in the Great Commandment (see Matt. 22:37-40). The same goes for sharing the gospel and multiplying disciples. We don't strive to bring people to the Lord or disciple people to earn favor with God or to get another notch on our spiritual belt. We've been entrusted with a mission, and we carry it out in love and obedience to glorify our Father in heaven.

This won't always be easy. We won't always feel motivated to share the gospel or to follow through by discipling a new believer. Sin continually draws us away from our mission. But Christ has promised His presence as we share His salvation. He said, "Remember, I am with you always" (Matt. 28:20) and "You will receive power when the Holy Spirit has come on you" (Acts 1:8).

THE POWER OF ONE

The common fear among believers—or the excuse among many believers—is that they aren't qualified or gifted as evangelists. Here are other excuses: "How can God use a big sinner like me to accomplish such a big task? How can just one person make such a big difference? Surely someone is more qualified than I."

Have you ever made these excuses? If not, what excuses have you made for not sharing your faith with others? Why?

How have you seen God use just one person to accomplish a monumental task?

The Bible illustrates that God often uses the power of one person to accomplish His work. In John, one adulterous Samaritan woman told her story to her town, and many came to believe in Jesus. In Genesis, one man trusted God by building a boat that saved humankind from destruction. In Exodus, one shepherd stood up against an Egyptian nation and delivered the Israelites from Pharaoh. In 1 Samuel, one boy conquered the Philistines when he killed their champion, Goliath. In Esther, one woman saw her nation spared from extermination when she courageously approached the king. In Acts, one fisherman preached a sermon that led three thousand people to be saved.

God can work the same way today. Here are some notable examples.

> One salesman and Sunday school teacher, Edward Kimball, led a young man named Dwight to Christ. Dwight Moody became a blazing evangelist who, it is said, led one million souls to Christ in his short lifetime. Wilbur Chapman received the assurance of his salvation after talking with Moody and went on to become a noted evangelist himself. The drunken baseball player Billy Sunday was an assistant to Chapman before becoming the most famous evangelist of his day. One of the fruits of Sunday's ministry was the forming of a group of Christian businessmen in Charlotte, North Carolina. This group brought the evangelist Mordecai Ham to Charlotte in 1934. A tall, awkward youth named Billy Graham was converted during those meetings. According to his staff, as of 1993, more than 2.5 million people had "stepped forward at his crusades to accept Jesus Christ as their personal Savior." Millions of souls trace their spiritual lineage back to the influence of one man, a simple Sunday school teacher, Edward Kimball.[4]

It's been said, "To the world you may just be one person, but to one person you may be the world."[5] The same holds true for your role as a Great Commission witness and multiplier. Your neighbor, peer, family member, coworker, or friend might appear to be just one lost soul. But to God, that may be the soul that helps lead millions to Himself.

Have you had the privilege of making a difference in one person's life? In what way?

Identify someone in your life with whom you could make a difference by sharing the gospel or helping to grow in discipleship.

Never underestimate God's plan for you and your witness as a Great Commission worshiper. No matter how incapable you might think you are, God is able.

VERBALIZING THE GOSPEL

So far in this study we've set the stage for you to share the gospel with unbelievers. In weeks 1–2 you practiced writing and sharing your formational and transformational testimonies. In week 3 we discussed the importance of strengthening your vertical and horizontal relationships to open doors for natural witnessing conversations. Last week we examined your call to be on mission with God and ways you can live a missional life.

Each week has highlighted the message of the gospel itself: that our Heavenly Father sent Jesus to live the life we should have lived and to die the death we all deserve to atone for the sin that separates us from God.

To you, what's the single biggest roadblock to your ability or willingness to verbalize the gospel? Why?

If all of these elements are precursors to communicating the gospel to unbelievers, how do you move forward in verbalizing it? The truth is that there's not a special script to follow. No formula, tract, or gospel presentation is equally effective for every circumstance. There's not just one way to verbalize the gospel; there are many ways. This is important because as you go on mission in your everyday life and relationships, no two gospel conversations will be the same.

Although learned methods for presenting the gospel might sometimes be helpful, depending on the situation, they might also be unhelpful. What happens when God gives you the opportunity to share with an unbeliever who grew up in church but abandoned it because the church abandoned him? "Admit, believe, and confess" may not be as effective as your testimony about how you were once abandoned by the church yourself. Your formational testimony at that point would become much more powerful than a method that someone else devised.

This is why it's so important for you to evaluate your past testimony, your current witness, and your relationships with unbelievers. God will direct you in your gospel conversation. You just have to be willing for Him to use you as He presents opportunities.

What are steps you can take to prepare yourself for different gospel conversations?

Review the testimonies you wrote in weeks 1–2. What path did God use to bring you to a point of surrender to His mission and to help you start growing spiritually? Who on your prayer list would benefit from hearing your formational and transformational testimonies?

Jesus encouraged His disciples as they embarked on His mission: "You will receive power when the Holy Spirit has come on you, and you will be My witnesses in Jerusalem, in all Judea and Samaria, and to the ends of the earth" (Acts 1:8). The apostle Paul encourages us as growing, multiplying disciples with similar words: "I pray that your participation in the faith may become effective through knowing every good thing that is in us for the glory of Christ" (Philem. 6).

Verbally sharing the faith was greatly important to Christ, just as it was to the early church. If we want to become obedient worshipers, we must be willing to share. As you go to the world, let God use you in each unique gospel conversation.

TODAY'S EVANGELISM EXPRESSION

Nothing will profoundly impact a Christian's life more than joining hands with the Holy Spirit and faithfully sharing the gospel of Christ. At that point what's natural becomes supernatural, and what's ordinary becomes extraordinary. If the person surrenders to Christ as Lord, he or she will never be the same.

Look over your prayer list of unbelievers. Look at their needs, their past struggles, and their current struggles. Start to determine what kind of conversation would be the most effective for each unbeliever. Ask God to lay the groundwork and start preparing you for a gospel conversation.

TODAY'S WORSHIP EXPRESSION

Read the Great Commandment (Matt. 22:37-40) and the Great Commission (Matt. 28:18-20) once more. Even in our imperfection God's allowed us to be a part of His mission to share the gospel throughout the world and to multiply disciples. Spend time in prayer asking Him to make you sensitive to spiritual needs around you and to give you courage to share the gospel. Ask Him also to show you how He can use you to disciple other believers.

DAY 4

CIRCLES OF INFLUENCE

What happens when you throw a rock into a still body of water? You see a ripple effect. The ripples might go on and on until they reach the edge of the water. It was this very image that led Oscar Thompson to conceive an evangelistic model called concentric circles.

Thompson was a pastor for 20 years and then a professor of evangelism. Before dying of cancer in 1980, he left a treasure of wisdom for those of us charged with sharing the gospel and making biblical disciples. Some of this wisdom was published in a popular book called *Concentric Circles of Concern*.[6] Thompson's approach, which viewed evangelism and discipleship as a singular entity, was transformational in light of the 1980s church-growth movement, which often valued numbers and additions over reproducing disciples.

Thompson's idea of relational evangelism helps us understand how God reaches people with the gospel through relationships. Thompson believed "He [God] wants to love your world through you and to draw it to Him."[7]

The diagram seen here, reproduced from Thompson's book, shows the radius of relationships in our lives. Each circle moving outward from the center represents a slightly more distant relationship in our circles of influence.

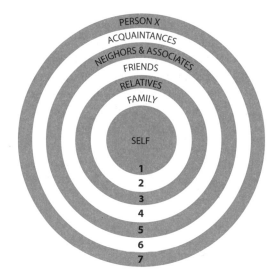

SELF

You, the Christian, occupy circle 1. To be an influence in circles 2–7, you must stabilize the nucleus. This doesn't mean circle 1 must be perfect in ability and knowledge before it can influence the other circles. It just means each believer must have a clear understanding of the gospel, know who they are in light of the gospel, and be willing to share it with people around them. Your influence on others flows from this sphere of self.

Examine the diagram. How does this concept affect the way you see your circles of influence?

Read Romans 12:6-8 and note how these verses address your personal responsibility to influence others. What gifts do you have that you could use to minister to others?

FAMILY, RELATIVES, AND FRIENDS

We're constantly surrounded by people we can influence with the message of Christ. Ranging from our immediate family to people we've never met (Person X), they fall into one of six concentric circles around us.

Although the intended focus of Thompson's approach was to encourage Christians to seek Person X intentionally, Thompson observed another more powerful phenomenon. He discovered that believers with a desire to share the gospel were most frequently reaching people in their first four circles—family, relatives, friends, and neighbors. He observed that this happened only when believers were willing to share the gospel with those they were closest to. Thompson concluded that we most effectively reach people through relationships.

Do you find that sharing the gospel is easier with the people you're closest to or with people you don't know well or at all? Why?

What are the major fears believers might have when approaching
someone they know well with the gospel?

"If our relationship with the Lord is genuine," Thompson wrote, "we will want
to share the good news of Christ with those closest to us."[8]

NEIGHBORS, ASSOCIATES, ACQUAINTANCES, AND PERSON X

Concentric circles 5–7 include neighbors, associates, acquaintances, and Person
X. Everyone in these circles represents someone we either know casually or
don't know at all. A constant awareness of intentionally living a missional life is
crucial in sharing the gospel within these three circles. Are you walking in step
with Christ? Is the love of Christ evident in the ways you interact with people? If
God gave you opportunities to engage in conversations with people from circles
5–7, will they encounter Him? These are all questions you should ask yourself in
preparation for gospel conversations.

List three examples of situations in which you could share
the gospel with people in circles 5–7.

1.

2.

3.

God wants to send forth an obedient army of responsible, committed worshipers
who want to reproduce themselves by proclaiming salvation to those without
Christ. It's crucial that we represent Christ's love by going on mission to people
in each of our circles of influence.

Many times the church fails at evangelism training. We teach people evangelistic
methods for reaching Person X and only Person X. Although reaching those we've
never met and will never meet again is wonderful, we sometimes fail to share with
and disciple the people we're closest to. Because we already have relationships in
these circles, we have greater opportunities to influence these people for Christ.

When God brings us in contact with someone, we're responsible for being on mission to that person. In one way or another, we're influencing people in all six circles of influence. Therefore, we should be evangelizing and making disciples in all six circles.

TODAY'S EVANGELISM EXPRESSION

Compare your prayer list of unbelievers to the concentric-circles diagram. Write names beside each circle of influence.

• Family:

• Relatives:

• Friends:

• Neighbors and associates:

• Acquaintances:

In which circles are you not demonstrating a God-honoring influence?

TODAY'S WORSHIP EXPRESSION

Read 1 Peter 3:15-16 and ask God to allow you to give a defense of the gospel of Jesus. Pray that God will give you opportunities to share this good news with the people you're influencing.

> Honor the Messiah as Lord in your hearts. Always be ready to give a defense to anyone who asks you for a reason for the hope that is in you. However, do this with gentleness and respect, keeping your conscience clear, so that when you are accused, those who denounce your Christian life will be put to shame.

DAY 5

CREATING GREAT COMMISSION WORSHIPERS

Yesterday we introduced the concept of concentric circles, developed by Oscar Thompson. Each circle of relationships in your life represents a group of people you're influencing. You might see them every day or only once in your lifetime. But God's brought you into contact with all of these people to be Christ's representative on earth. He calls you to multiply yourself as a reproducing Great Commission worshiper in each person's life.

Thompson also outlined a seven-stage process for making genuine disciples of the individuals in your circles of influence.

STAGE 1: GET RIGHT WITH GOD, SELF, AND OTHERS

Thompson said, "A person can never lead another closer to the Lord than he or she already is. Evangelism must flow from a life that's deeply in love with the Lord."[9] Thompson believed the most important word in the English language is *relationship*. If love is the train, he said, relationship must be the track.

According to Thompson, evangelism is supremely relational. The most important relationship is our relationship with God. We must come to God on His terms, make Him the Lord of our lives, and receive His gift of salvation. Once we're right with God, we need to examine our relationships with others and restore them if necessary. No one can be right with God and still tolerate broken relationships. In fact, we're called to be reconcilers in the world:

> If anyone is in Christ, he is a new creation; old things have passed away, and look, new things have come. Everything is from God, who reconciled us to Himself through Christ and gave us the ministry of reconciliation: That is, in Christ, God was reconciling the world to Himself, not counting their trespasses against them, and He has committed the message of reconciliation to us. Therefore, we are ambassadors for Christ, certain that God is appealing through us. We plead on Christ's behalf, "Be reconciled to God."
>
> 2 Corinthians 5:17-20

How does God's reconciling us to Himself encourage us to be reconciled with others?

Record the name of someone with whom you need to restore a relationship. What's a specific way you'll reach out to him or her?

STAGE 2: SURVEY YOUR RELATIONSHIPS

In this stage Christians are encouraged to examine their circles of relationships to identify individuals who need Christ's love and salvation. You should have taken this step at the end of day 4. We may not realize how many people God has put within our reach. Once we start to identify these individuals, we should gather basic information that will guide our prayers and our efforts to reach out to them.

Which of your circles represents the largest number of unbelievers? Why?

Identify some needs of unbelievers in those circles that you could pray for and help meet.

STAGE 3: WORK WITH GOD THROUGH PRAYER

Prayer isn't a warm-up exercise for the spiritual work of evangelism, worship, and discipleship. It's intimate fellowship with a holy God who desires close, frequent prayer time with His children. Through these intimate times He will give you discernment to recognize opportunities for making disciples and wisdom to know what steps to take.

Over the past few weeks how has God already answered some of your prayers for the lost people in your circles of influence?

STAGE 4: BUILD RELATIONAL BRIDGES TO PEOPLE

As you pray for the people in your concentric circles, you'll learn to recognize unsaved individuals. In response you should intentionally begin to build bridges to the people God has put in your path. You do this by getting to know them, learning their needs, and showing your concern for their needs. This enables God's love to flow through you with the goal of leading them to Christ.

This is how Paul described building relational bridges in 1 Corinthians 9:19-22:

> Although I am a free man and not anyone's slave, I have made myself a slave to everyone, in order to win more people. To the Jews I became like a Jew, to win Jews; to those under the law, like one under the law—though I myself am not under the law—to win those under the law. To those who are without that law, like one without the law—not being without God's law but within Christ's law— to win those without the law. To the weak I became weak, in order to win the weak. I have become all things to all people, so that I may by every possible means save some.

What did Paul mean when he said, "I have become all things to all people" (v. 22)?

Name a couple of ways you can make yourself a slave to someone or become weak "in order to win the weak" (v. 22).

STAGE 5: SHOW GOD'S LOVE BY MEETING NEEDS

When you show God's love to a needy world through compassionate ministry and sacrificial service, you give visual evidence that He's working in your heart to love people you otherwise might not seek to know. Meanwhile, He's working in those you're praying for and connecting with so that you'll become a conduit of His unending love as He draws hurting people to Himself.

Read Matthew 25:35-40. How is our love for others evidence of our love for God?

STAGE 6: MAKE DISCIPLES AND HELP THEM GROW

As we witness for Christ and share our faith, the Holy Spirit convicts lost people of sin and shows them the truth of the gospel. If they choose to yield to Christ, we and other Christians need to help them develop their personal relationship with Christ through consistent prayer, Scripture reading, and other spiritual disciplines.

Remember that evangelism is meshed with discipleship. You can't have one without the other. The Great Commission doesn't just command us to go. We're commanded to make disciples, baptize them, and teach them how to follow Christ. We must show and teach new believers key Christian disciplines, basic Christian beliefs, the importance of serving, how to have a quiet time, the priority of church involvement, and how to become a Great Commission worshiper.

Is there someone you've led to the Lord who needs to be discipled? What could you do to disciple this new believer?

STAGE 7: HELP NEW CHRISTIANS MAKE DISCIPLES

The final stage begins the cycle for the next generation of new Christians. Once someone becomes a Christ follower, encourage them to survey the people in their concentric circles. They should begin praying for them, mending broken relationships, building relational bridges, and showing God's love in practical ways. The ultimate goal is for new believers to multiply disciples by leading others to Christ and by leading them to become authentic disciples and worshipers:[10]

> How can they call on Him they have not believed in? And how can they believe without hearing about Him? And how can they hear without a preacher? And how can they preach unless they are sent? As it is written: "How beautiful are the feet of those who announce the gospel of good things!" So faith comes from what is heard, and what is heard comes through the message about Christ.
>
> Romans 10:14-15,17

To become a Great Commission worshiper, we must intentionally reproduce new worshipers. This doesn't occur by accident. It's an intentional process of obeying Christ's call to go and make disciples.

TODAY'S EVANGELISM EXPRESSION

By this point you should be actively seeking to lead lost people to Christ by serving them, developing relationships with them, and praying for them. This week intentionally share the good news of Jesus with at least one person you've been praying for and serving. Expect God to work through your witness and prayer so that you'll soon have an opportunity to disciple a new believer in Christ.

TODAY'S WORSHIP EXPRESSION

Pray throughout the day that God will give you a heart for the lost. Pray that He will generate a passion in you to see the lost come to saving faith in Christ.

Read Paul's words and spend a moment praising God that He's entrusted you to share His gospel:

> I am not ashamed of the gospel, because it is God's power for salvation to everyone who believes, first to the Jew, and also to the Greek. For in it God's righteousness is revealed from faith to faith, just as it is written, "The righteous will live by faith."
>
> Romans 1:16-17

1. W. Henrichsen, *Disciples Are Made, Not Born* (Carol Stream, IL: Victor Books, 1979), 140–41.
2. John Avant, *If God Were Real* (New York: Howard Books, 2009), 64.
3. Ibid., 68.
4. Dave Earley and David Wheeler, *Evangelism Is* (Nashville: B&H, 2010), 133–34.
5. Brandi Snyder, Search Quotes [online, cited 16 October 2012]. Available from the Internet: *www.searchquotes.com.*
6. Summaries of Thompson's ideas in days 4–5 are summarized from W. Oscar Thompson Jr., *Concentric Circles of Concern: Seven Stages for Making Disciples* (Nashville: B&H, 1999). LifeWay offers a Bible study that lays out and applies Thompson's principles. Order *Growing Disciples: Witness to the World*, item 005085767.
7. W. Oscar Thompson Jr. with Carolyn Thompson Ritzmann, *Witness to the World* (Nashville: LifeWay, 2008), 9.
8. Thompson, *Concentric Circles,* 20.
9. Thompson and Ritzmann, *Witness to the World,* 9.
10. Thompson, *Concentric Circles,* 35. In reference to stages 1–7, see pages 30–34.

WEEK 5 GROUP EXPERIENCE

Use the following activity to introduce the topics covered in this week's study.

SUPPLIES NEEDED. A small tub of Play-Doh® or modeling clay for each participant

ACTIVITY. Look around the room and identify an object you find interesting. This object can be anything that's observable within the room, including people, chairs, books, clocks, purses, and so on. Once you've identified your object, spend three to five minutes attempting to reproduce it with your Play-Doh. After you've finished, allow others to guess which object you were attempting to reproduce.

After everyone has finished guessing, discuss the following questions.

What emotions did you experience while attempting to reproduce your object? Why?

What emotions do you experience when you think about making disciples for God's kingdom? Why?

What did you like best about the material in week 5? Why?

What questions would you like to discuss as a group?

Prepare for further group discussion by reading aloud the following passage.

> Look, I'm sending you out like sheep among wolves. Therefore be as shrewd as serpents and as harmless as doves. Because people will hand you over to sanhedrins and flog you in their synagogues, beware of them. You will even be brought before governors and kings because of Me, to bear witness to them and to the nations. But when they hand you over, don't worry about how or what you should speak. For you will be given what to say at that hour, because you are not speaking, but the Spirit of your Father is speaking through you.
>
> Matthew 10:16-20

Use the following excerpts from the study material to move below the surface and engage in transformational conversations.

DAY 1. A disciple is someone who follows Christ. So seeing someone acknowledge and believe Jesus died in their place for the forgiveness of their sins isn't enough. We must make disciples by teaching them how to follow Christ.

This is the most overlooked and underappreciated element of Great Commission worship. Someone can be submitting to God's formational and transformational work and living a relational and missional life but still fall short of Great Commission worship if they don't understand what it means to reproduce by making disciples.

What ideas or images come to mind when you hear the word *discipleship?* Why?

When you were a new believer, who helped you know what it means to follow Christ?

The most common excuses for not sharing Jesus are a fear of rejection and a false belief that without experience and knowledge, the witness can't be effective. Nothing could be further from the truth.

When have you been tempted to use these excuses in order to avoid the responsibility of making disciples?

DAY 2. Some church members move through life with little regard for the needs of hurting people. Their concept of worship and evangelism is limited to the church building on Sunday morning. They're conditioned to be indifferent because they lack biblical discipleship that challenges them to reproduce their faith. They believe ministry is the responsibility of paid staff members, not of everyday Christians. They're loyal to the institution of the church as long as it doesn't interfere with their daily lives.

What emotions do you experience when you read the previous statements? Why?

Because disciples are called to reproduce more disciples, evangelism and discipleship depend on each other. Therefore, evangelism is much more than sharing gospel presentations and seeking decisions. Discipleship is much more than simply training people to memorize Bible verses. Neither the process of evangelism nor the process of discipleship is complete unless it intentionally meshes with the goal of leading the person who's evangelized to become a reproducing worshiper.

In your own words, explain the relationship between evangelism and discipleship.

In what ways does your church connect evangelism and discipleship? In what ways can that connection improve?

DAY 3. So how do we go about communicating the gospel to an unbeliever? The truth is that there's not a special script to follow. No formula, tract, or gospel presentation is equally effective for every circumstance. There's not one just way to verbalize the gospel; there are many ways. This is important because as you go on mission in your everyday life and relationships, no two gospel conversations will be the same.

What methods of sharing the gospel have you recently used?

What's the role of the Holy Spirit in our gospel conversations?

DAY 4. God wants to send forth an obedient army of responsible, committed worshipers who want to reproduce themselves by proclaiming salvation to those without Christ. It's crucial that we represent Christ's love by going on mission to people in each of our circles of influence.

As a group, review Oscar Thompson's concentric-circle model of evangelism. In what ways does the model help you?

What opportunities exist for you to share the gospel with your friends and family?

What opportunities exist for you to share the gospel with neighbors, associates, and acquaintances?

DAY 5. Prayer isn't just a warm-up exercise before you do the spiritual work of evangelism, worship, and discipleship. It's intimate fellowship with a holy God who desires close, frequent prayer time with His children. Through these intimate times He will give you discernment to recognize opportunities for making disciples and wisdom to know what steps to take.

How often do you set aside time to pray for people in your circles of influence who've not yet experienced Christ as Savior?

What obstacles currently prevent you from spending more time in prayer on behalf of those who need Christ? How can those obstacles be overcome?

APPLY TO LIFE
Discuss your experiences with the Evangelism Expression and Worship Expression at the end of each day's study material.

Describe your recent attempts to share the gospel with those who need to hear it. What surprised you about the experiences?

Do you feel qualified to disciple another follower of Christ? Why or why not?

Read Romans 1:16-17. As a group, express thanks to God for entrusting us with the privilege of sharing the gospel.

PRAY
Read aloud Acts 4:23-31. Pray that God will grant you opportunities to share the gospel in the coming week. Also pray that God will grant you boldness to confidently share the good news of salvation without fear or doubt.

BECOMING A GREAT COMMISSION WORSHIPER

You might have heard the common saying "It's good to plan ahead. It wasn't raining when Noah built the ark."

Likewise, Great Commission worshipers must make plans for the eventual storm. We must plan for the challenges we'll face as we go into the world to share the good news of Christ and disciple new believers to become reproducing worshipers. Philip Schaff talks about how this happened in the early church:

> While there were no professional missionaries devoting their whole life to this specific work, every congregation was a missionary society, and every Christian believer a missionary, inflamed by the love of Christ to convert his fellow men. Every Christian told his neighbor, the laborer told his fellow laborer, the slave to his fellow slave, the servant to his master and mistress, the story of his conversion as a mariner tells the story of the rescue from shipwreck.[1]

What if we had the same passion about the message God's entrusted to us? Believers must remind themselves of the centrality of the gospel and its eternal implications for their lives and for people in their circles of influence.

This study has given you a discipleship model for going on mission and making disciples. The gospel is the driving force behind this multiplying process, and its focus is directed outward toward others. This week will offer final preparation for living your life as a Great Commission worshiper.

DAY 1

A BIBLICAL MODEL OF WORSHIP

In Genesis 22 God commanded Abraham to take his only son, Isaac, to the land of Moriah and sacrifice him on an altar. When they reached the site, Abraham gave these instructions to his servants: "Stay here with the donkey. The boy and I will go over there to *worship;* then we'll come back to you" (v. 5, emphasis added).

Outside the biblical arena Abraham's actions would appear to be those of a lunatic. How could anyone rationalize killing his child by calling it worship? Abraham used the term because worship isn't an event or something we do for God. It's an act of unbridled obedience to God, even when rational explanations are hard to come by. Abraham was willing to give God his full obedience, even if it meant sacrificing his precious son.

In many cases Christians admit their need to worship, but they stop short of being radical, passionate followers of Christ. They settle for outward expressions of worship with little regard for what it means to be a multiplying disciple of Jesus Christ. Generations of anemic worship have resulted in an impotent faith that reduces worship to an act of personal expression and ignores Jesus' command to share the gospel. As a result, these believers can't get motivated to share their faith with an unbelieving family member, neighbor, or friend.

Would you describe your worship of God as passionate or anemic? Why?

Worship is one of the most frequently communicated terms among believers today but, at the same time, one of the most misunderstood. As we go into the world as Great Commission worshipers, it's crucial that we have a scriptural understanding of worship that we practice and share with others.

Let's look at some characteristics of true worship we've discovered in this study.

WORSHIP IS MORE THAN A WORSHIP SERVICE. It's common to confuse doing church with being the church. If worship becomes something that occurs only at a specific time and location each week, we lose God's call to be worshipers as we journey through daily life. The heartbeat of worship is a daily response of obedience to the commands of Christ, which leads us to join Him on mission.

What differences would be evident in your life if you viewed worship as a lifestyle?

WORSHIP LEADS TO EVANGELISM. Some people think an emphasis on worship precludes a responsibility to evangelize. But if worship is an obedient response to God's commands for every believer, every valid expression of worship should be done with the aim of multiplying God's kingdom through evangelism.

PUBLIC AND PRIVATE WORSHIP ARE INTEGRALLY RELATED. If believers see no relationship between their public and private worship, they're flirting with hypocrisy. What resides in the heart will ultimately reveal itself in attitudes and actions. However, public and private worship aren't interchangeable. Without regular times of private devotion, public worship will become perverted and shallow. Private worship is the foundation of genuine public worship.

In what ways is private worship foundational to corporate worship?

How would you currently compare your private and public worship?

WORSHIP IS ABOUT TOTAL OBEDIENCE. Many modern churches and believers equate worship and music, but they aren't synonymous. Worship isn't being entertained by talented musicians but surrendering to a holy God. Worship also doesn't refer to a musical style, such as blended, contemporary, or traditional. Rather, it's a surrendered approach to life.

Do you normally think of worship as obedience or something completely different? Explain.

WORSHIP INCLUDES PREACHING. Some people believe worship occurs only when music is present. Although music is an important aspect of worship, it's the proclamation of God's Word that brings people to repentance and transforms their lives.

WORSHIP IS BASED ON TRUTH. Many people believe worship is based on their personal experiences, so if they don't conjure the right feelings, they think they haven't worshiped. However, worship centers on the Person of Christ, not on personal feelings. Jesus said we must "worship in spirit and truth" (John 4:24). Emotions change, but the truth of God's Word remains the same. Real worship brings about real change.

Describe a time when you experienced real and lasting change during a time of worship.

Based on what you've read, list three things worship is and isn't.

Worship Is	Worship Isn't
1.	1.
2.	2.
3.	3.

A PICTURE OF WORSHIP

Paul captured many of these biblical truths about worship in his letter to the Romans:

> Oh, the depth of the riches
> both of the wisdom and the knowledge of God!
> How unsearchable His judgments
> and untraceable His ways!
> For who has known the mind of the Lord?
> Or who has been His counselor?
> Or who has ever first given to Him,
> and has to be repaid?
> For from Him and through Him
> and to Him are all things.
> To Him be the glory forever. Amen.

> Therefore, brothers, by the mercies of God, I urge you to present your bodies as a living sacrifice, holy and pleasing to God; this is your spiritual worship. Do not be conformed to this age, but be transformed by the renewing of your mind, so that you may discern what is the good, pleasing, and perfect will of God.

> Romans 11:33–12:2

This biblical picture of worship reminds us that although all things belong to God, the ultimate purpose for His people is to bring Him "glory forever" (11:36). This is why we live and worship: so that God can be eternally exalted among the nations through the surrendered, obedient lives of His people.

What are you communicating to God by your current level of obedience?

From what kind of attitude or motivation should our obedience come?

Worship doesn't end here. Paul implores us to present our bodies "as a living sacrifice, holy and pleasing to God; this is your spiritual worship" (12:1). In other words, our greatest act of worship isn't blindly responding to God as an act of compliance to a set of rules and standards. On the contrary, God requires that if His children are to be genuine worshipers, we must be transformed by allowing Him to renew our minds. Only then can we reveal to the unredeemed world the "good, pleasing, and perfect will of God" (12:2).

How is your spiritual transformation into the likeness of Jesus pushing you outward to express God's will in the world?

TODAY'S EVANGELISM EXPRESSION

Biblical worship always drives us to unite with Christ in ministry. Real disciples are called to join Christ as He goes on mission to bring the world to Himself.
- Name one way God has shaped your understanding of worship through this study.
- Name one way your worship of God could influence the unbelievers with whom you're sharing the gospel.
- Name one way you'll present your body "as a living sacrifice, holy and pleasing to God" (Rom. 12:1) as an act of worship to God this week.

TODAY'S WORSHIP EXPRESSION

Spend 10 minutes in prayer asking God to show you ways you aren't believing His Word. Ask Him to reveal times you could be worshiping Him but aren't. Leave time to listen to what God has to say.

DAY 2

A BIBLICAL MODEL OF EVANGELISM

Many things can trip us up as evangelists of the gospel. We're either too lazy, too busy, or—perhaps the biggest reason of all—too fearful. Maybe we're afraid our delivery of the gospel will do more harm than good. Maybe we're afraid we'll come across as arrogant. Perhaps we're afraid we won't know the answers to difficult questions. But most of all, we fear rejection.

In 2 Timothy 1:7-10 the apostle Paul stated:

> God has not given us a spirit of fearfulness, but one of power, love, and sound judgment. So don't be ashamed of the testimony about our Lord, or of me His prisoner. Instead, share in suffering for the gospel, relying on the power of God.
>
> > He has saved us and called us
> > with a holy calling,
> > not according to our works,
> > but according to His own purpose and grace,
> > which was given to us in Christ Jesus
> > before time began.
> > This has now been made evident
> > through the appearing of our Savior Christ Jesus,
> > who has abolished death
> > and has brought life and immortality to light
> > through the gospel.

Fear is rational in certain situations, but according to Scripture, it shouldn't apply to the charge of evangelism. Because God has equipped us with a spirit of "power, love, and sound judgment" (v. 7), we should urgently go into a helpless world with the good news of Jesus. Longtime speaker and seminary professor Howard Hendricks once said, "In the midst of a generation screaming for answers, Christians are stuttering."[2]

In what ways are you stuttering? What current or past fears have kept you from sharing the gospel?

UNDERSTANDING BIBLICAL EVANGELISM

Yesterday we looked at a biblical view of worship. Today let's make sure we have a biblical understanding of evangelism.

EVANGELISM IS A MANDATE. Some Christians seem to think evangelism is optional. Maybe that's why so few share their faith. Jesus said, "You will receive power when the Holy Spirit has come on you, and you will by My witnesses in Jerusalem, in all Judea and Samaria, and to the ends of the earth" (Acts 1:8). As written in the original Greek language, the phrase "you will be My witnesses" is a direct command of Christ.

List ways you or your church is involved in reaching your Jerusalem, Judea, Samaria, and ends of the earth.

Jerusalem—home, neighborhood, and community:

Judea—county and state:

Samaria—country:

Ends of the earth—throughout the world:

EVANGELISM REFLECTS A TRANSFORMED LIFE. There are hundreds of ways to share Christ, but evangelism isn't just sharing the right information. You can't divorce Jesus' message from the life He lived. He not only shared the truth but also embodied the truth through His lifestyle. Similarly, the knowledge you share is validated through a consistent testimony of a changed life.

In what ways does a believer's life support sharing the gospel?

Identify any practice in your life that invalidates your witness. How does that practice limit your effectiveness in sharing the gospel?

EVANGELISM IS EVERYONE'S ASSIGNMENT. Although some Christians have gifts, abilities, and personalities that make it more natural for them to share, the call to evangelize is for every believer. The word *evangelism* means *good news* or *the message*. So evangelism isn't merely sharing the good news; it *is* the good news. Because evangelism is the good news of Christ, every Christ follower must embrace sharing the good news as a lifestyle.

EVANGELISM GOES HAND IN HAND WITH DISCIPLESHIP. Some people justify their discomfort with evangelism by saying, "I'm a disciple maker, not an evangelist." The truth is that evangelism and discipleship are dependent on each other. Although intentional evangelism that leads to spiritual conversion always precedes the process of discipleship, neither process is complete until the one being discipled learns to multiply his witness by sharing Christ.

EVANGELISM IS DIFFERENT FROM PRAYER. Make no mistake: prayer is an essential component of evangelism. There's no way to be effective in evangelism without a deep, abiding relationship with God in prayer. However, to pray for the lost without sharing the message of Christ stops short of the target. Usually, when believers earnestly pray for their unsaved friends and family, their burden increases to the point that they're compelled to share Christ boldly with them.

How have your prayers motivated you to share Jesus with unbelievers?

A PICTURE OF EVANGELISM

Jesus calls us to yield our lives in service to Him and to others through evangelism and discipleship. Consider His words:

> The hour has come for the Son of Man to be glorified. I assure you: Unless a grain of wheat falls to the ground and dies, it remains by itself. But if it dies, it produces a large crop. The one who loves his life will lose it, and the one who hates his life in this world will keep it for eternal life. If anyone serves Me, he must follow Me. Where I am, there My servant also will be. If anyone serves Me, the Father will honor him.
>
> John 12:23-26

What did Jesus mean when He said, "The one who hates his life in this world will keep it for eternal life" (v. 25)?

How does the picture of wheat apply to being a reproducible Great Commission worshiper?

Biblical evangelism requires a life that's totally sold out and obedient to the Master. A grain of wheat that's died and been buried can yield a large crop, continually reproducing itself. Otherwise, it's nothing more that an impotent grain of wheat. In the same way, holding on to your life will make you useless to the kingdom of God. But if you're willing to die to yourself and join Christ on mission every day, He will produce a large crop through you as a reproducible Great Commission worshiper.

TODAY'S EVANGELISM EXPRESSION

Jesus went out into the harvest field, meeting people where they were and investing in their lives. One source says Jesus made contact with 132 people in the Gospels. Six of those were in the temple and 4 in the synagogues. The other 122 contacts were made in the field of life.[3] Jesus sends us into the harvest field as well.

Describe how you're acting on or preparing for the challenge presented at the end of week 5 to share the gospel with at least one person.

Evangelism must never be reduced to something you perform as a duty to God. Rather, like breathing, it should be an involuntary response to naturally share Christ whenever possible. In short, evangelism is the essence of who you are as a Christ follower walking through daily life. It's the consistent, natural overflow of a deep and abiding relationship with Christ.

Since beginning this study, have you grown in your ability to share Christ as a part of your daily life? If not, what's holding you back?

TODAY'S WORSHIP EXPRESSION

Commit yourself to becoming a Great Commission worshiper who's so much in love with Jesus, so committed to the worship of Jesus, and so devoted to obeying every command of Jesus that you can't restrain yourself from telling others about your incredible relationship with the Son of the living God. Pray today that God will give you that passion and will continue to remove fears and hindrances that keep you from the mission of spreading His fame and glory.

DAY 3

LIVING AS A GREAT COMMISSION WORSHIPER

There's a sad reality facing Christianity. It wouldn't be far-fetched to claim that throughout the history of the church, at no other time have Christians been more educated but less effective than we are today. Numerous reasons can be given for this decline, but a primary reason is the lack of emphasis on discipleship.

Genuine discipleship should always reproduce followers of Jesus who have a passion to fulfill the Great Commission, not mere students of knowledge, seekers of guidance for a better life, and practitioners of institutional religion. Without reestablishing the cycle of multiplication that combines discipleship with evangelism and worship, the church will continue to decline into indifference and apathy. Jesus expects all of His children to share His heart for reaching the world with the gospel. Therefore, genuine disciples are those who take on the attributes of Jesus and actively participate in the Great Commission by following Him.

List all of the attributes of Jesus that you can think of.

Which of those attributes are weakest in your life and thus preventing you from being an effective follower of Jesus?

PUT ON CHRIST

Throughout this study we've looked at many passages in which Jesus called us to make disciples. The most obvious and most quoted is the Great Commission, in which Jesus gave a clear charge to His disciples and assured them of His continued spiritual presence (see Matt. 28:18-20). John's Gospel also has a condensed version of Jesus' commissioning His disciples: "As the Father has sent Me, I also send you" (John 20:21). And in the Book of Acts, Luke recorded Jesus' final instructions to His disciples before ascending to heaven: "You will receive power when the Holy Spirit has come on you, and you will be My witnesses in Jerusalem, in all Judea and Samaria, and to the ends of the earth" (Acts 1:8). Jesus' words directly call us to follow Him and make reproducing disciples.

In what ways have you answered Jesus' call to go and make disciples since beginning this study?

Jesus used the phrase "Follow Me" at least 20 times in the New Testament. The first time He said it was probably to Philip (see John 1:43). In Matthew 4:19 Jesus told Simon Peter and his brother, Andrew, "Follow Me, … and I will make you fish for people!"

One way those who follow Christ are called to reproduce disciples is through a character and a lifestyle that are Christlike—that emulate Christ. The apostle Paul said to "put to death what belongs to your worldly nature: sexual immorality, impurity, lust, evil desire, and greed, which is idolatry. Because of these, God's wrath comes on the disobedient" (Col. 3:5-6). In place of sinful practices, we should put on the attributes of Christ.

Read Colossians 3:1-3. How do we put to death corrupt things and put on the attributes of Christ?

Read Colossians 3:12-17. What attributes does Paul instruct us to put on?

In our study we've also looked at the Great Commandment (Matt. 22:37-40). When a religious leader asked Jesus, "Which command in the law is the greatest?" (v. 36), Jesus thoughtfully responded by first pointing to the need to love "the Lord your God with all your heart, with all your soul, and with all your mind" (v. 37). He added that the second most important command is to love "your neighbor as yourself" (v. 39).

Jesus' brief response conveyed the heart of both worship and evangelism. He called us to glorify God with unyielding allegiance, but we haven't fulfilled the calling until we go beyond the immediate circle of self to love our neighbors as ourselves. If we fall in love with Christ and seek to glorify His name, we'll also love the people who cross our path each day. For either command to be fulfilled, self must fall to the bottom of the list in our daily priorities.

Worship, then, isn't an isolated act or a staged event. It's a passionate response to the heart cry of God that includes active participation in the Great Commission. But Great Commission worship isn't just something you do. It's something you are.

You don't have to be told to love and care for family members. You naturally have those desires as part of who you are. Similarly, when you take on the attributes of Christ, you naturally respond in obedience to the Great Commission and the Great Commandment.

What attributes of Christ are you naturally expressing because of your relationship with Him?

What attributes don't come as naturally to you as a follower of Christ?

True worshipers should naturally desire to wrap their faith in flesh that daily lives out the gospel in every sphere of life. The result should be a life that's consumed by worship and fueled by obedience to Christ's call to become reproducible fishers of people (see Mark 1:17).

ATTRIBUTES OF CHRIST

Countless attributes of Christ should compel us to become reproducible fishers of people. Putting on these characteristics will prepare us to go out as Great Commission worshipers. Here are a few of those attributes.

HUMILITY. Jesus submitted to His Father by leaving His home and coming to ours. He was faithful to the mission to which He was called: "to seek and to save the lost" (Luke 19:10). We too have been called to faithfulness in our mission as followers of Jesus. One way we can faithfully follow Him is to humble ourselves by dying to self daily. Take a look at Jesus' example:

Make your own attitude that of Christ Jesus,
who, existing in the form of God,
did not consider equality with God
as something to be used for His own advantage.
Instead He emptied Himself
by assuming the form of a slave,
taking on the likeness of men.
And when He had come as a man
in His external form,
He humbled Himself by becoming obedient
to the point of death—
even to death on a cross.

Philippians 2:5-8

Name two ways a humble attitude would strengthen
your effectiveness as a Great Commission worshiper.

1.

2.

SACRIFICE. Are you withholding anything from God? Are you sacrificing
yourself for His mission? As the perfect and ultimate sacrifice, Jesus gave His life
as a ransom for our sin. He said, "The Son of Man did not come to be served, but
to serve, and to give His life—a ransom for many" (Matt. 20:28). We respond to
Jesus' call by sacrificing our comfort for the sake of His kingdom.

Read these passages and identify what Jesus called us to do.

Luke 9:23

Luke 9:59-60

Luke 14:33

In what way have you sacrificially served someone in your circles
of influence this week?

STEADFASTNESS. Jesus is steadfast in His love for us. He's constant in His forgiveness to us. And while He was on earth, He was unwavering in His Father's mission to save us from our sin. His hope is that we'll continue His mission with this same attitude. The author of Hebrews encourages us this way:

> Since we also have such a large cloud of witnesses surrounding us, let us lay aside every weight and the sin that so easily ensnares us. Let us run with endurance the race that lies before us, keeping our eyes on Jesus, the source and perfecter of our faith, who for the joy that lay before Him endured a cross and despised the shame and has sat down at the right hand of God's throne. For consider Him who endured such hostility from sinners against Himself, so that you won't grow weary and lose heart.
>
> Hebrews 12:1-3

When are the times in life when you feel most like giving up?

How does Jesus serve as your example as you go on mission?

Our mission won't always be easy. We'll experience pain, hardship, suffering, and trials of many kinds, but Jesus challenges us to keep our focus on obedience to Him: "If you continue in My word, you really are My disciples" (John 8:31).

TODAY'S EVANGELISM EXPRESSION

As you think about your task of sharing the gospel, answer the following questions.
- What are the biggest challenges to sharing the gospel with the individuals you've been praying for?
- Have you taken those challenges to God in prayer?
- How are you integrating your personal testimonies of formation and transformation into your witness?

TODAY'S WORSHIP EXPRESSION

Reflect on the three attributes of Jesus mentioned today and praise Him for the ways those have influenced your life. Think of specific examples of ways Jesus has demonstrated His humility, sacrifice, and steadfastness for you.

DAY 4

EXECUTING WORSHIP AND WITNESS

Although God is the only One who can change lives, He graciously gives us hidden strength, intestinal fortitude, and empowerment for joining His work of worship and witness. The following passages are just two of many in God's Word that encourage the people of God to carry out His mission boldly and fearlessly:

> I want you to know, brothers, that what has happened to me has actually resulted in the advance of the gospel, so that it has become known throughout the whole imperial guard, and to everyone else, that my imprisonment is in the cause of Christ. Most of the brothers in the Lord have gained confidence from my imprisonment and dare even more to speak the message fearlessly.
>
> Philippians 1:12-14

> We have this treasure in clay jars, so that this extraordinary power may be from God and not from us. We are pressured in every way but not crushed; we are perplexed but not in despair; we are persecuted but not abandoned; we are struck down but not destroyed. We always carry the death of Jesus in our body, so that the life of Jesus may also be revealed in our body. For we who live are always given over to death because of Jesus, so that Jesus' life may also be revealed in our mortal flesh.
>
> 2 Corinthians 4:7-11

Peter and John boldly spoke the Word of God and were unified by the gospel. Moses experienced this same boldness when appearing before Pharaoh. God granted this kind of boldness to a shepherd boy, David, when standing before the giant. It's this same sense of boldness that Elijah demonstrated on Mount Carmel when, as the Spirit of God was on him, he confronted and defeated 450 prophets of Baal. This boldness characterized the apostle Paul when he stood on Mars Hill and proclaimed the truth about the unknown god. This type of boldness enabled the disciples to stand before rulers and kings and proclaim the gospel without fear. And it's this same boldness that God wants to give you and me as Great Commission worshipers.

God doesn't give us a spirit of fear (see 2 Tim. 1:7). Rather, God gives us a spirit of bold confidence that comes only when we walk and work with the power of God in our lives.

Identify someone you know who walks with a spirit of boldness as he or she carries the gospel to the world. Why do you consider that person bold?

Why is a spirit of confidence and boldness important as we go on mission?

Today we'll explore three ways our worship and evangelism should be executed with the boldness God provides.

FOCUSED INTENTIONALITY

First, our worship and evangelism should be executed with focused intentionality. If we're going to experience the transformed lifestyle of a Great Commission worshiper, our worship of God and labor of evangelism must be done with one intentional purpose: to glorify God. We must be preoccupied with God. Our worship habits, work ethic, evangelistic endeavors, and Kingdom building must begin with deliberate, planned intentionality.

Name three ways someone can be intentional in pursuing a transformed lifestyle of worship and witness.

1.

2.

3.

Robert J. Morgan tells a story about a man who dreamed an angel escorted him to church one Sunday:

> There he saw the keyboard musician playing vigorously, praise team singing, the musicians playing their instruments with gusto. But the man heard no sound. The congregation was singing, but the sound was utterly muted. When the minister rose to speak, his lips moved, but there was no volume. In amazement, the man turned to his escort for an explanation.
>
> "This is the way it sounds to us in heaven," said the angel. "You hear nothing because there is nothing to hear. These people are engaged in the form of worship, but their thoughts are on other things and their hearts are far away."[4]

If we're building relationships, witnessing, ministering, worshiping, and discipling with a spirit of intentionality, our thoughts, motives, attitudes, and activities will reflect the glory of God. Although we'll thrill at the reality of God's blessings, the credit of success will go to God alone.

Name a way you can be more intentional about the things you're doing for the Kingdom.

HUMILITY AND SURRENDER

Second, our worship and evangelistic efforts should be executed with humility and surrender. Humility comes as we give credit for any success to God and God alone. The Book of Proverbs provides a principle we should apply to our own achievements, victories, and accomplishments:

> Let another praise you, and not your own mouth—
> a stranger, and not your own lips.
>
> Proverbs 27:2

Name one area of your life in which you're prone to personally accept credit instead of giving glory to God.

Read the following passages and list the way each speaks to that area of your life.

Psalm 25:9

Ephesians 2:8-9

James 4:6

Executing ministry with humility and surrender may be the most difficult. Pride runs deep in the hearts of churches and individuals. Remember that the ultimate goal is to glorify our Maker in heaven. This can't be done if we put ourselves first.

ETERNITY IN VIEW

Third, our worship and evangelism efforts should be executed with eternity in view. At the end of the day, the church doesn't need another songbook, worship set, worship video, or praise team leading the latest songs about God. The church doesn't need another event or goal-driven evangelism program. The church needs believers who see the lost with an eternal perspective. Our worship, witness, discipleship, missional lifestyle, and service should flow from that perspective.

How would you describe your current perspective on your worship and witness?

What would happen if Christ were physically with us now? Would our worship be intentional? What if we saw the wounds in His hands? Would we humbly fall on our faces before Him and confess our sins? Would our church practice business as usual, or would we passionately seek the lost with eternity in view?[5]

How do you answer the previous questions? Why?

If Christ were physically present in our church or our homes, we'd experience focused intentionality. We'd long to serve, be quick to make amends with our brother and sister, and be eager to fill our pews and offering plates. The reality is, Christ is with us. We know this because He promised He would be:

> I will ask the Father, and He will give you another Counselor to be with you forever. He is the Spirit of truth. The world is unable to receive Him because it doesn't see Him or know Him. But you do know Him, because He remains with you and will be in you.
>
> John 14:16-17

How have you experienced the Holy Spirit's presence in your recent efforts to worship and witness?

Loving God and loving others are expressions of worship, and they're of utmost importance to a reproducing discipleship process. Everything in this process connects to the lifeline of exalting God above all else. As you go and execute Great Commission worship, think of it like a car frame. As the frame of a car provides needed stability and protection, worship provides a similar foundation on which a new believer can become a reproducing disciple. Worship is a constant track from which true disciples and disciple makers must never stray.

How are you beginning to see the discipleship process play out in the lives of people you've shared the gospel with?

TODAY'S WORSHIP EXPRESSION

Consider fasting for a day during the next week. This could be as simple as not eating lunch one day so that you can use that time to pray for someone you're sharing the gospel with or discipling. During that time thank God that He's put this person in your circle of influence. Pray for his or her openness to the gospel, as well as for your own intentionality, humility, surrender, and eternal perspective in relating to that person.

DAY 5

A LIFELONG GREAT COMMISSION WORSHIPER

Having reached the end of our study, we should be well equipped to carry out our God-given mission as Great Commission worshipers. The purpose of this study is to take you through a discipleship process that will help you develop essential knowledge, skills, and attributes for becoming a Great Commission worshiper. From the time a person gives his or her life to Christ, a new worshiper needs to embrace the Great Commandment to love God and to love others, as well as the Great Commission to go and make disciples. As we've seen, these concepts grow directly from the words of Jesus.

If the purpose of life is to exalt Christ as obedient worshipers, it makes sense that loving God should be the primary motivation of all Christians and that loving others must become the primary mission. We continually engage in these lifelong callings to multiply Christ's kingdom.

Name some practical ways to love others.

Think back to your salvation experience. Who demonstrated the kind of love Jesus described in the Great Commandment? Describe the impact it had on you.

Let's conclude our study with a final look at the five major elements of Great Commission worship and a final charge for going on mission to our world.

A FINAL LOOK

We explored five components of our worship and witness. Let's review what these mean as we look forward to integrating them into our daily lives.

FORMATIONAL. Worship and witness are active experiences that shape us into Great Commission worshipers of our Creator. And as we glorify God, we're simultaneously conformed to His image.

When we pray in faith, devote time to God's Word, and live a life of obedience and service, God will not only increase our desire to do those things but will also continually form us into Christlikeness. Great Commission worship is formational.

How has God conformed you to the image of His Son as you've obeyed His call to worship and witness?

TRANSFORMATIONAL. When we engage with the power of the Holy Spirit, He fuels our growth and transforms our lives. Believers should be prepared to share their transformational stories with people in their circles of influence.

The Holy Spirit is ready and able to produce changed lives. He changes broken and damaged vessels into worshipers and witnesses of the living God. As we're transformed into His likeness, we're equipped to teach, encourage, and communicate the gospel to those at different points in their spiritual journeys. Great Commission worship is transformational.

What have you experienced in sharing your transformational story? If you haven't shared your story, what's holding you back?

RELATIONAL. God created us to enjoy meaningful relationships. He longs for a relationship with His children. As we worship, our vertical relationship with the Father grows. He also expects us to create and nurture horizontal relationships with both believers and unbelievers. As we cultivate our vertical and horizontal relationships, God strengthens us as Great Commission worshipers and gives us opportunities to share the good news and make disciples.

Life is about relationships—with God and with others. As our relationships grow, we're equipped to worship God and witness to others. Great Commission worship is relational.

What's one hindrance that's keeping you from a healthier relationship with God? With other people?

MISSIONAL. Our desire to be a Great Commission worshiper is evident in the way we respond to God's call for us to go on mission. We carry out this call in our daily lives. The gospel of Christ should infiltrate every aspect of life and thrust us into missional living.

When we become followers of Christ, He sends us out into the world as His ambassadors (see 2 Cor. 5:20). He wants us to demonstrate and share His salvation with those in our circles of influence—at home, at work, in our neighborhoods, and throughout the world. Great Commission worship is missional.

Name the specific arenas of influence you currently have. How is your life reflecting the gospel in each one?

REPRODUCIBLE. The natural progression of Great Commission worshipers' development is to reproduce themselves in the lives of others. This is done when the evangelized becomes an evangelizer and when the discipled becomes a discipler. The Great Commission must not stop with going. This circular, dynamic process will create fully functioning disciples who go and make Great Commission worshipers.

Reproduction is essential for multiplication to take effect. As we go into the world, follow Christ, and make disciples, we teach others to do the same. Great Commission worship is reproducible.

Have you started reproducing other disciples? If not, what's one step you can take to get started?

A FINAL CHARGE

Can we be true worshipers of Christ if we ignore the commands of the Great Commission to go and make disciples? Can we be biblical disciples without multiplying new Great Commission worshipers? It's past time for the church to stop compromising on what it means to be a genuine disciple of Christ. God fully expects all of His children to grow in Christ and to multiply. That's why we're called the body of Christ. Paul wrote:

> He personally gave some to be apostles, some prophets, some evangelists, some pastors and teachers, for the training of the saints in the work of ministry, to build up the body of Christ, until we all reach unity in the faith and in the knowledge of God's Son, growing into a mature man with a stature measured by Christ's fullness. Then we will no longer be little children, tossed by the waves and blown around by every wind of teaching, by human cunning with cleverness in the techniques of deceit. But speaking the truth in love, let us grow in every way into Him who is the head—Christ. From Him the whole body, fitted and knit together by every supporting ligament, promotes the growth of the body for building up itself in love by the proper working of each individual part.
>
> Ephesians 4:11-16

Just as your cells naturally reproduce to sustain life and grow, members of the body of Christ are called to grow and reproduce.

Jesus' Great Commandment and Great Commission call us to be authentic disciples throughout our lives on earth. That means we can't compartmentalize the concepts of worship, evangelism, and discipleship. Each function is essential and equally important for creating a genuine follower of Christ. The result will be a fully committed, reproducing worshiper who joyfully and intentionally shares the wonders of God with a hurting and sinful world.

May the words of the psalmist echo in our hearts as we go out to proclaim the greatness of our Lord:

> Shout joyfully to God, all the earth!
> Sing about the glory of His name;
> make His praise glorious.
> Say to God, "How awe-inspiring are Your works! …
> All the earth will worship You
> and sing praise to You.
> They will sing praise to Your name."
> Come and see the wonders of God;
> His acts for humanity are awe-inspiring.
> Come and listen, all who fear God,
> and I will tell what He has done for me.
>
> Psalm 66:1-5,16

With whom is God convicting you to share His wonders? How will you respond?

The church needs—and God is seeking—men and women who are totally devoted to Him, full of love for God because of what Christ has done on the cross, transformed by the work of the Holy Spirit in their lives, and passionately motivated by their worship to tell the good news of Jesus Christ to everyone they meet. The church needs men and women who want to make a difference in the lives of people for eternity. The church needs men and women who live and breathe Great Commission worship. They live their lives for the glory of God and the testimony of Jesus Christ. It's a lifelong calling, and its results will resonate throughout eternity.

Which element of Great Commission worship resonated most as you studied it? Why?

In which area do you believe God is calling you to be a more obedient participant?

TODAY'S EVANGELISM EXPRESSION

The foundation has been set, and the charge has been given. Now you must act to go and make disciples. Commit to the multiplying process. If you haven't already started discipling those you've led to Christ, follow through by beginning that process. Teach them how to follow Christ. Teach them basic spiritual disciplines. Stress the importance of involvement in and ministry through a local church. Encourage personal witnessing. In short, prepare them to become reproducing Great Commission worshipers.

TODAY'S WORSHIP EXPRESSION

Read Psalm 27:1-4 and thank God for the salvation that comes through His Son. Thank Him for His continued, faithful presence in your life. Ask Him to empower you for the mission you've been called to as a formed, transformed, relational, missional, and reproducing Great Commission worshiper.

> The LORD is my light and my salvation—
> whom should I fear?
> The LORD is the stronghold of my life—
> of whom should I be afraid?
> When evildoers came against me to devour my flesh,
> my foes and my enemies stumbled and fell.
> Though an army deploys against me,
> my heart is not afraid;
> though a war breaks out against me,
> still I am confident.
> I have asked one thing from the LORD;
> it is what I desire:
> to dwell in the house of the LORD
> all the days of my life,
> gazing on the beauty of the LORD
> and seeking Him in His temple.

1. Philip Schaff, *History of the Christian Church,* volume 2, *Anti-Nicene Christianity* (Grand Rapids: Eerdmans, 1910), 20–21.
2. Howard Hendricks, *Taking a Stand: What God Can Do Through Ordinary You!* (Portland, OR: Multnomah Press, 1983), 12.
3. J. K. Johnston, *Why Christians Sin* (Grand Rapids: Discovery House, 1992), 142.
4. Robert J. Morgan, *Preacher's Sourcebook of Creative Sermon Illustrations* (Nashville: Thomas Nelson, 2007), 809.
5. Karen Burton Mains, *Sing Joyfully* (Carol Stream, IL: Tabernacle, 1989), 3–6.

WEEK 6 GROUP EXPERIENCE

BREAK THE ICE
Use the following activity to introduce the topics covered in this week's study.

SUPPLIES NEEDED. A laptop or TV with a DVD player

ACTIVITY. Watch a movie excerpt featuring a motivational speech or inspiring moment—something that would excite people. Movies that contain such moments include *Facing the Giants*, *Courageous*, *Unconditional*, and others.

When the clip is over, discuss the following questions.

What motivates you to live as a Great Commission worshiper? What excites you about doing so?

How has this study increased your motivation to help others experience the joy of worshiping and glorifying Christ?

Describe what you liked best about the material in week 6. Why?

What questions would you like to discuss as a group?

Prepare for further group discussion by reading aloud the following passage.

> The hour has come for the Son of Man to be glorified. I assure you: Unless a grain of wheat falls to the ground and dies, it remains by itself. But if it dies, it produces a large crop. The one who loves his life will lose it, and the one who hates his life in this world will keep it for eternal life. If anyone serves Me, he must follow Me. Where I am, there My servant also will be. If anyone serves Me, the Father will honor him.
>
> John 12:23-26

DIG DEEPER
Use the following excerpts from the study material to move below the surface and engage in transformational conversations.

DAY 1. *Worship* is one of the most frequently communicated terms among believers today but, at the same time, one of the most misunderstood. As we go into the world as Great Commission worshipers, it's crucial that we have a scriptural understanding of worship that we practice and share with others.

Throughout the course of this study, what have you learned about worshiping God?

What words best describe your experiences of worshiping God in recent weeks?

Although all things belong to God, the ultimate purpose for His people is to bring Him "glory forever" (Rom. 11:36). This is why we live and worship: so that God can be eternally exalted among the nations through the surrendered, obedient lives of His people.

What's your reaction to the previous statements? Why?

DAY 2. Biblical evangelism requires a life that's totally sold out and obedient to the Master. A grain of wheat that's died and been buried can yield a large crop, continually reproducing itself. Otherwise, it's nothing more that an impotent grain of wheat. In the same way, holding on to your life will make you useless to the kingdom of God. But if you're willing to die to yourself and join Christ on mission every day, He will produce a large crop through you as a reproducible Great Commission worshiper.

What does it mean to die to yourself as a follower of Christ?

How does the process of dying to ourselves affect our efforts at evangelism?

In what ways are evangelism and worship connected? How is that connection reflected in your life?

DAY 3. One way those who follow Christ are called to reproduce disciples is through a character and a lifestyle that are Christlike—that emulate Christ. The apostle Paul said to "put to death what belongs to your worldly nature: sexual immorality, impurity, lust, evil desire, and greed, which is idolatry. Because of these, God's wrath comes on the disobedient" (Col. 3:5-6). In place of sinful practices, we should put on the attributes of Christ.

Countless attributes of Christ should compel us to become reproducible fishers of people. Putting on these characteristics will prepare us to go out as Great Commission worshipers.

As a group, list all of the attributes of Christ you can think of.

Which of these attributes would you most like to demonstrate in your life? Why?

What obstacles are currently preventing you from demonstrating those attributes more fully? How can you overcome those obstacles?

DAY 4. Our worship and evangelism should be executed with focused intentionality. If we're going to experience the transformed lifestyle of a Great Commission worshiper, our worship of God and labor of evangelism must be done with one intentional purpose: to glorify God. We must be preoccupied with God. Our worship habits, work ethic, evangelistic endeavors, and Kingdom building must begin with deliberate, planned intentionality.

How can we be intentional in pursuing a transformed lifestyle of worship and witness?

If Christ were physically present in our church or our homes, we'd experience focused intentionality. We'd long to serve, be quick to make amends with our brother and sister, and be eager to fill our pews and offering plates. The reality is, Christ is with us. We know this because He promised He would be.

Read John 14:16-17. What emotions do you experience when you hear these words?

How have you experienced the Holy Spirit's presence in your efforts to worship and witness?

DAY 5. Can we be true worshipers of Christ if we ignore the commands of the Great Commission to go and make disciples? Can we be biblical disciples without multiplying new Great Commission worshipers? It's past time for the church to stop compromising on what it means to be a genuine disciple of Christ. God fully expects all of His children to grow in Christ and to multiply. That's why we're called the body of Christ.

Read Ephesians 4:11-16. Where do you fit in the body of Christ?

What steps will you take in the coming weeks to move forward as a Great Commission worshiper?

APPLY TO LIFE

Discuss your experiences with the Evangelism Expression and Worship Expression at the end of each day's study material.

What obstacles and challenges have you recently faced while attempting to share the gospel and make disciples?

How can you connect your efforts at evangelism and discipleship with those of your local church?

Read Psalm 27:1-4. As a group, thank God for His power and support for living as Great Commission worshipers.

PRAY

End this study with a time of confession, followed by commitment. Confess any lingering doubts or fears preventing you from fully engaging as a Great Commission worshiper. Finish by verbally expressing to God your commitment to serve His kingdom and to glorify Him through worship, evangelism, and discipleship.